D0065981

Praise for *Global Dexterity*

"Thought-provoking with a practical application. *Global Dexterity* provides critical tools for adapting to a different culture while maintaining one's authenticity. A definite must-have for every HR professional given our global and culturally dynamic workforce."
—Patricia Francisco, Director of Human Resources, CRA/LA-DLA, successor to the former CRA/LA

"Whether you're traveling abroad, studying internationally, relocating for work, or welcoming foreign employees to your team, *Global Dexterity* is a must-read for anyone seeking to become a true global citizen. It offers a refreshing perspective that minimizes the focus on mimicking cultural norms to fit in and maximizes the importance of adapting to new experiences without losing the essence of who you are."
—Lisa B. Sousa, General Counsel, EF Education First

"*Global Dexterity* provides a clear road map to conquer the quest for cultural diversity, which is critical in today's flat world. The self-assessments on identifying cultural gaps and working on a personal mind-set to overcome them will prove handy to anyone working in a new cultural environment."

—Mansi Madan Tripathy, Chief Marketing Officer,
Shell India

"Andy Molinsky does a masterful job of demystifying the challenges one faces working in or with other cultures. His book is as insightful as it is practical. In a world in which you need to both understand and adapt to cultural differences, this is the book to read."

—Matthias Kempf, Director, HR Talent Europe,
adidas Group

GL🌐BAL
DEXTERITY

**How to Adapt Your Behavior across Cultures
without Losing Yourself in the Process**

GL⊕BAL
DEXTERITY

ANDY MOLINSKY

Harvard Business Review Press

Boston, Massachusetts

The web addresses referenced in this book were live and correct at the time of the book's publication but may be subject to change.

Library of Congress Cataloging-in-Publication Data

Molinsky, Andy.
  Global dexterity: how to adapt your behavior across cultures without losing yourself in the process / Andy Molinsky.
     pages cm
  ISBN 978-1-4221-8727-2 (alk. paper)
  1. International business enterprises—Management—Cross-cultural studies. 2. Management—Cross-cultural studies. 3. Corporate culture—Cross-cultural studies. 4. Intercultural communication. 5. Diversity in the workplace. 6. Business etiquette. I. Title.
  HD62.4.M64 2013
  395.5'2—dc23
                                                    2012041299

The paper used in this publication meets the requirements of the American National Standard for Permanence of Paper for Publications and Documents in Libraries and Archives Z39.48-1992.

ISBN: 978-1-4221-8727-2
eISBN: 978-1-4221-8728-9

For Jen, Alice, and Ben:
with love and gratitude

Contents

CONTENTS

PART THREE
Fine-Tuning Your Global Dexterity

Preface

Have you ever lived or worked abroad and had to adapt your behavior to be successful in a new cultural setting? Are you planning on working abroad and curious about how to develop the skills to be effective in your new assignment? Do you lead or manage people who live or work abroad and whose success is critical to the success of your organization? If the answer to any of these questions is yes, this book is for you.

Global Dexterity is about learning to adapt your behavior across cultures—no matter what culture you come from, what culture you are going to, or the situation you find yourself in. The purpose of the book is to develop the ability to smoothly and successfully adapt how you act in a foreign setting—so that you are effective and appropriate in that setting without feeling that you are losing yourself in the process. The tools and frameworks that you will learn about in this book come from my decade-long research program about the challenges that managers, executives, and employees face when adapting behavior across cultures and from a popular MBA elective course that I have created to help people overcome these challenges, which manifest themselves in a wide variety of different situations and contexts. For example:

- You're from the United States and are working in Germany. You need to communicate negative feedback to colleagues much more assertively and directly than you would ever do in the United States.

- You're from China and are working in the United States. You need to disclose more personal information when making small talk with someone you do not know than you ever would in China.

- You are Japanese and are working in France. You need to speak your mind more assertively at a meeting with your boss than you ever would have done in Japan.

To be effective in situations such as these, you need to adapt. You need to learn to act outside of your personal comfort zone. But adapting your behavior across cultures is often easier said than done. You can feel anxious and embarrassed about not knowing exactly how to behave, and inauthentic and disingenuous about how awkward and unnatural it feels. You can feel frustrated and annoyed about having to adapt in the first place. Such feelings can be quite a burden. They can leak into your behavior and cause you to act inappropriately. They can also make you want to avoid situations where you have to adapt in the first place—even situations that are important to your professional success.

So, is there a solution? Can you learn to adapt your behavior without feeling like you are losing yourself in the process? It sounds impossible, and that's what I initially thought when I first started working on this topic many years ago. However, what I have learned over the past ten years of researching, interviewing, teaching, and working with a wide variety of professionals from a range of different cultural backgrounds is that it's not. You can learn to have your cake and eat it too when adapting behavior in a foreign setting.

This book is for anyone interested in improving his or her ability to function more effectively in a foreign cultural setting, no matter the culture you come from, the culture you are going to, or the situation you find yourself in. It's filled with stories and anecdotes of people who have been able to come up with creative ways of adapting their behavior and remaining authentic at the same time—of *fitting in without giving in*—in situations you would think would be very hard to manage in this way. You will learn how an American-born CEO working in India was able to devise a way of blending his own preference for a bottom-up, participative style of leadership with the reality that Indian subordinates typically expect and respond more positively to a more top-down, authoritarian style. You will see how a Russian-born consultant in the United States was able to be far more assertive with her boss in the United States than she ever would have been in Russia, but in a way that actually felt consistent with her cultural ideals. You will meet people from Germany, Brazil, China, South Korea, Israel, and the United Kingdom—people from all sorts of different cultural backgrounds who were able to devise creative ways of adapting to different cultures.

I wrote this book because I believe that there is a serious gap in what has been written and communicated about cross-cultural management and what people actually struggle with on the ground. Until now, the vast majority of writing about culture in business has focused on educating people about *differences* across cultures. For example, you might learn that Swedes are more individualistic than Chinese, or that Germans tend to schedule, arrange, and manage time whereas Mexicans and Indians are more apt to treat time more fluidly. The logic is that if people can learn about cultural differences, they can adapt their behaviors successfully. And for some people, that's true. Some people are so skilled at managing themselves across cultures that you might call them "cultural chameleons." They are able to seamlessly blend, unconsciously it seems, and at each turn function smoothly and successfully according to the new cultural norms.

For the rest of us, however, especially those of us who are, for lack of a better term, *monoculturals*—born and raised in a single cultural environment and now trying to function effectively in another culture—cultural adaptation isn't always so seamless. We might possess knowledge of cultural differences, but we can struggle as we attempt to put this knowledge into practice. That's where this book comes in. It teaches people who are not bicultural or multicultural by birth how to act effectively in different cultural environments and at the same time to feel authentic, or authentic enough, when doing it.

In this book, you will learn what global dexterity is and why it is a critical skill for you to master, what challenges you will likely encounter when attempting to develop your own global dexterity, and how you can overcome these challenges by learning to customize your own personal approach toward cultural adaptation.

The lessons in this book are applicable to anyone from any culture doing business in any situation—whether on a

long-term or short-term assignment overseas, or simply working with people from a different culture in one's native country.
The technique is both universally applicable and customizable.
That is, this is not a one-size-fits-all system. The techniques
you'll learn will allow you to adapt your own cultural behavior
in a way that works for you. The goal is to help you learn to
modify your behavior in a way that does not feel like you are, as
one of the people I have worked with memorably put it, "committing a crime against your own personality."

How I Came to This Book

I first became interested in the subject in the late 1990s, during
my PhD studies at Harvard, when I volunteered at a resettle-
ment agency in Boston to help immigrant professionals from
the former Soviet Union find jobs in the United States. These
were smart people with excellent résumés. The problem most
of them had was cultural: they simply could not master the
American-style assertive and self-promotional behavior necessary for job interviews and networking with employers. In fact,
what was most enlightening to me about this experience was
that it wasn't the knowledge that they lacked: they all could tell
me how you had to behave in the United States and how that
differed so significantly from Russia. The problem was translating this knowledge into behavior.

For example, I recall one woman—an extremely experienced
engineer with many different graduate degrees in Russia; extensive, relevant work experience; and excellent English—who
continuously failed at promoting herself in the American interview. She knew what to do, but felt "silly" and "foolish" making

small talk (in Russia, interviews were much more professionally focused only), and felt anxious and embarrassed about her
inability to successfully adapt. She told me how much these
emotions weighed on her as she attempted to switch her behavior and how difficult that psychological experience was for her.

I continued to pursue this interest at my first job as a professor at the University of Southern California, where I encountered a similarly challenging situation of cultural adaptation.
We had many bright, talented, and motivated foreign MBA students from East Asian cultures such as China, Taiwan, Korea,
and Vietnam who were reluctant to contribute their thoughts
to classroom discussions and debates, which were an essential
part of the MBA program, and which also happened to count
for a large percentage of their final grade. These students were
motivated, worked extremely hard, and knew how they were
supposed to participate in class. But for some reason, they
were unwilling—or unable—to actually do it and contribute
their ideas. Like the Russians, they struggled to translate what
they knew intellectually into effective cross-cultural behavior.

When I turned to the academic literature to solve this puz-
zle, I came up empty. Instead of offering advice about how
people could overcome cultural differences and learn to adapt
behavior in light of cultural differences, what people were
focusing on was the differences themselves: how Chinese were
different from Russians, or how Russians were different from
Japanese. There was little about how people could successfully
overcome these differences and learn to adapt their behavior.

In the years since these two formative experiences, I have
studied and worked with a wide range of people from the
United States and abroad learning to adapt their cultural

behavior in a variety of different foreign settings. In each case, I have found the essential challenge to be the same: knowledge of cultural differences is certainly necessary to be effective abroad, but it is not sufficient. To be truly effective in foreign cultures, you need to develop the global dexterity necessary for translating your knowledge into effective behavior.

Armed with an understanding of these processes and with a passion to try to make a difference in the lives of the many foreign-born professionals I have met throughout the years, I began crafting a set of tools based on my academic research to give people the courage and the skills to develop their own global dexterity. The book you have in your hands is the result of this work.

What's in This Book

Let me say a few words about the stories and examples you will read about in this book. The vast majority of stories are actual events, as told to me by people I have interviewed or worked with, albeit with a few details changed to protect anonymity. A small percentage of stories do not come from one specific source, but are anecdotes that I have crafted to reflect insights from many different people I have studied or worked with throughout the years. I begin each of these composite narratives with "Imagine that . . . " or "Imagine the following . . . " to distinguish them from stories told to me by a specific individual.

In all cases, the material is deeply grounded in years of serious study about global dexterity. For the book alone, I have conducted over seventy interviews with professionals about their experiences adapting cultural behavior and about the norms for appropriate behavior in specific countries and cultures. The book is also based in my own decade-long research program about global dexterity at Harvard University, the University of Southern California, and Brandeis University. Finally, the book is also influenced by the many informal conversations that I have had throughout the years with managers and executives at roundtable discussions and seminars, as well as from teaching and working with foreign-born MBA students. I am particularly indebted to these students for the hundreds of conversations we have had about cultural adaptation. These discussions have been invaluable in helping me craft these ideas around global dexterity and translate them into a series of actionable tools.

Let me also say a brief word about how cultural differences are portrayed in this book. Throughout, you will see examples of cultural differences: that Indians tend to communicate less directly than Germans or that Israelis tend to communicate more directly than Americans, and so on. When I speak about these cultural differences, I am describing *prototypical* cultural differences, by which I mean the average or typical differences you will find within a population. In other words, if you took the entire population in Israel and were somehow able to assess their communication style, the average style would be more direct than the average communication style of all Americans. I don't mean to suggest that *all* Israelis are more direct than *all* Americans or that *all* Indians are less direct than *all* Americans. That's simply not true. For example, many Indians actually have a quite direct communication style—perhaps as a result of having lived or worked in the West or from having worked for a multinational company in India. Similarly, plenty of Israelis are less direct than some Americans. So, when I talk about cultural differences in the book, it's in the spirit of prototypes, rather than stereotypes. These differences do exist on average—as you will hear from talking with natives of these countries or from consulting the academic literature. But they do not necessarily define how any particular individual person from a given culture will behave.

My hope is that this book can be a useful resource to help you make better sense of the foreign experiences you have had and to help you have more successful experiences in the future. To that end, at the conclusion of each chapter, I provide a series of personalized tools that you can use to directly apply the lessons from that chapter to your own experience.

I hope I've given you a good sense of what's included in the book and have whetted your appetite for more. I'd also like to give you a quick sense of what's *not* included in the book. First, although language is clearly a key issue when crossing cultures, this book is not a language book. I do not talk a great deal about language and the difficulties associated with mastering a foreign language, even though this is clearly a key part of learning to function effectively in a new cultural setting—something I experienced firsthand as a non-native student in Spain and a working professional in France. I also do not provide detailed rules for how to behave appropriately in every cultural situation you will find yourself in. Believe me, I'd love to do that!—but it's obviously impossible. What I do provide you with, however, is a method and set of frameworks that you can apply to any situation you face.

Finally, although you will find examples throughout the book from both men and women, I do not focus particularly on gender itself as an issue in intercultural interaction. I understand and appreciate how women in particular may face special challenges when adapting their behavior across cultures, especially in countries with very different gender roles than their own. From studying this issue for many years and from talking with women about their experiences overseas, my sense is that at a broad level, the framework that I present in this book accounts for these gender issues. For example, women might feel resentful or angry about having to adapt to a set of behaviors that a female manager would never have to accommodate to in her native cultural setting. Or women in other situations might feel tremendously inauthentic and disingenuous acting in a way that is not only atypical of their native culture, but that also violates their deeply held values and beliefs about how to interact with the opposite gender. These core reactions to the act of switching cultural behavior are not only covered in the book, but are the essence of the framework that I put forth.

I'd like to end this preface with a quote from an American executive who truly understood the importance of cultural adaptation. In making the case for the importance of developing cultural competence, Jack Welch, the former CEO of General Electric, said:

> The Jack Welch of the future cannot be like me. I spent my entire career in the United States. The next head of General Electric will be somebody who spent time in Bombay, in Hong Kong, in Buenos Aires. We have to send our best and brightest overseas and make sure they have the training that will allow them to be the global leaders who will make GE flourish in the future.[1]

Do you see what Welch is getting at? He is not necessarily saying that to be successful you need to have a multicultural upbringing. He's saying that through different experiences in foreign cultural settings, you can develop the global dexterity to be successful. Jack Welch clearly believed in the importance of global dexterity, and I imagine that if you have picked up this book, you also understand its critical importance in today's business world. So take the leap; start to learn how to operate successfully in a world where cultural differences require changes in behavior. My sincere hope is that this book can be a key building block in your own process of developing global dexterity.

Acknowledgments

I am very grateful to so many friends and colleagues who have helped shape and hone the ideas in this book. First, I would like to thank Richard Hackman, who inspired me to write a book in the first place, and who has always been an inspiration for the type of scholar that I aspire to become. Very early in my career, Richard taught me to study what I care about, what interests me, and what might make a difference in the lives of others. I feel so lucky to have had him as my mentor.

Throughout the years I have also received tremendous assistance and feedback from my academic colleagues who have helped me develop and hone my ideas about cross-cultural adaptation, both in this book and in the pages of academic articles. These colleagues include: Paul Adler, Nalini Ambady, Mary Yoko Brannen, Joel Brockner, May Dabbagh, Jane Dutton, Marshall Ganz, Adam Grant, Judy Hall, Sally Maitlis,

Tsedal Neeley, Joyce Osland, Mike Pratt, Ruth Wageman, and Joyce Wang; my business and psychology colleagues at Brandeis—in particular, Ben Gomes Casseres, Sandra Cha, Jane Ebert, Bruce Magid, Brad Morrison, and Detlev Suderow; members of the Boston-area Groups Group seminar at Harvard University; and participants at the yearly "May Meaning Meeting" group who provided such a supportive and collegial atmosphere for helping me develop these ideas.

I also, of course, owe a debt of gratitude to the many managers, employees, and executives who took time out of their schedules to openly discuss their experiences of cultural adaptation with me. You made this book possible, and I am grateful for your candor and generosity. As part of the writing of this book, I spoke with more than seventy people from around the globe—working professionals from Mexico, Brazil, Canada, the United Kingdom, France, Germany, Italy, Switzerland, Russia, India, Nigeria, Korea, China, Japan, Vietnam, Israel, the United Arab Emirates, and the United States. I found these people through my own contacts as well as through those of my generous colleagues Mark Blecher, Greg Chen, Adam Grant, Sujin Jang, Lynne Levesque, Mark Mortensen, Amy Sommer, and Xin Wang.

Many of the people I spoke with will remain anonymous because I have used their direct stories. However, others whose experiences do not appear in the book but who provided valuable background information about cultural differences include: Mat Abramsky, Adedotun Adebiaye, Noor Al Jallaf, Michel Anteby, Murtala Bagana, Cicero Baggio, Mati Balan, Yoni Balan, João Banzato, Lilia Bikbaeva, Max Blythe, Neel Bungaroo, Andy Carter, Greg Chen, Lu Chen, Jose Chong, Nick Christ, George Chu, Harland Chun, Ilan Dee, Drew

Denker, Faustine Ehringer, Markus Englhardt, Miguel Gonzalez, Barbara Guenther, Alice Gur-Arie, Karim el Quasri, Bob Green, Hideaki Hirata, Jenny Jiang, Zhenling Jiang, Boris Kapeller, Daniel Kim, Jay Kim, Phillippe Le Corre, Juan Lepe, Pedro Llamas, Yong-Taek Min, Gowri Nagaraj, Ije Nwokomah, Azuka Okofu, Paolo Orozco, Jane Pedersen, Claudia Peus, Dan Pfau, Ergys Prenika, Nan Qu, Bernhard Radtke, Kalpesh Ramwani, Steve Rochlin, Rami Sarafa, Christina Sevilla, Simon Sherrington, Sarah Stuart, Allan Tamen, Perry Teicher, Nils Tessier du Cros, Eric Teung, Jeff Thelen, Toby Uzo, and Michael Zakkour. I also want to thank the hundreds of foreign- and American-born MA and MBA students I have taught and worked with at Brandeis International Business School. You have provided me with tremendous insight into the dynamics of cultural adaptation and with a "living laboratory" for helping me develop and hone these ideas.

There are many other important people who made this book possible. My editors at Harvard Business Review Press, Melinda Merino and Courtney Cashman, have provided insightful and encouraging feedback throughout the process and have truly been a pleasure to work with. I also want to thank Nihan Celiktas, Debi Choudhury, Jen Molinsky, Steve Molinsky, Beth Schinoff, and Jessy Wang for providing outstanding feedback on earlier drafts of the manuscript, and Bill Bliss for providing key insights into the book-writing process at just the right times.

Finally, this book could never have been possible without the support and encouragement of my family—my mother and father, my brother and my sister-in-law, my in-laws, and my own family and children. My father in particular, given his own publishing expertise writing textbooks that teach English as a second language, has been a tremendous source of wisdom at all phases of this project, providing ongoing feedback about all sorts of issues and always willing to take time out of his own busy schedule to help me. My brother, Eric, who is an accomplished public radio producer and storyteller, has been a great resource as well, especially about how to tell a good story and connect with an audience. And, finally, my wife, Jen, has been the best partner a book-writing husband could ever ask for. She has supported and encouraged me throughout this process, provided insightful and encouraging feedback on countless versions of my ideas, and most important, always believed in me. I never could have written this book without her.

To everyone who contributed to this book: I am forever grateful.

PART ONE

Why Global
Dexterity Matters

In this first section of the book, you'll learn what global dexterity is and why it matters. You will meet Eric Rivers, the American-born CEO of an Indian technology firm in Mumbai, who is thoughtful, knowledgeable, and highly motivated to work effectively in India, but who struggles when switching his behavior to an Indian cultural style. You will meet Feng Li, a Chinese-born management consultant for a major American-based professional services firm in Chicago, who knows that he needs to participate in brainstorming sessions with partners in order to succeed, but who has trouble speaking up, despite the fact that he is highly knowledgeable and has many useful points to contribute. You will meet many others like Eric and Yu who struggle not with learning about cultural differences, but with the ability to actually translate this knowledge into effective behavior—what I call global dexterity. The first chapter explains why global dexterity is so critical in today's global economy, and in the second chapter, I explain why, despite its great importance, global dexterity can be such a challenging skill to master.

CHAPTER 1

Introduction to Global Dexterity

Eric Rivers was pacing back and forth in his office. He poured himself a cup of coffee but then immediately threw it out; the tea was much better in Mumbai. Eric asked his assistant to get him a cup of chai, then decided to take a walk around the neighborhood to clear his head. He passed by a brand-new school, a few businesses selling t-shirts and electronics, and a large open construction site where two elderly men were walking their cows the way Eric used to walk his dog back in Los Angeles. It had been three months since Eric had moved to Mumbai, and he was still getting used to it all.

Eric had been hired six months earlier to lead the division of a global consulting firm offering strategic advice to technology firms in the fast-growing Indian market. He saw amazing possibilities for what he could achieve; that was why he decided to forgo more conventional work opportunities in the United States.

Eric felt like he was doing everything right in his attempt to adapt to the Indian cultural environment. A seasoned leader with extensive management experience in the West, he was eager to bring his American management philosophy to this vibrant developing economy. His philosophy had two key elements. The first was empowerment, which Eric felt was a universal idea that transcended cultural boundaries. In the past, Eric had worked for many different bosses, and the ones he respected the most had worked hard to inspire their workers to succeed by giving them opportunities to develop skills, make decisions for themselves, and contribute to the firm. Eric also deeply believed in a flat hierarchy: in being highly collaborative and involving his employees in as much of the decision making process as possible.

Eric put his philosophy into action as soon as he arrived in Mumbai. First, instead of taking an office with a door in the corner of the building as he noticed other managers in the building had done, he took a cubicle right in the "trenches" with his fellow employees. That way he would not be seen as an arm's-length, unapproachable leader, but as someone who was willing to get his hands dirty and figure things out with the team. Eric also decided to engage his employees in the process of making key strategic decisions. One of Eric's best managers in Los Angeles would always involve her employees in the strategic decision-making process. Rather than pretending that she had all the solutions, she would include employees as she herself was trying to work through challenging strategic issues. Her view was that employees who were often closest to the "action" also had very important ideas to contribute to the discussion. Also, by involving them in the process, she could help mentor employees in the process of how to make a decision, which she believed was a valuable skill to teach anyone. Thus, whenever his Indian employees came to Eric with a problem, Eric patterned his approach after his mentor's. He would not pretend that he had all the answers; instead, he would invite them into the decision-making process.

Eric was eager to put these powerful management techniques into action. He was passionate about engaging with his Indian workers, getting them thinking for themselves, and, most importantly, letting them know that they were part of the team.

The only problem was that his vision didn't work. In fact, it failed miserably. Unlike his former employees in the United States, who relished the chance to make their own decisions and who saw Eric as more of a colleague than a boss, Eric's Indian workers interpreted this freedom as a lack of competence and confidence on *Eric's* part as a manager. After all, why would a leader sit with his employees and keep asking their opinions about important leadership matters? He must lack the ability to do it himself. Rather than being energized and engaged by Eric's empowerment initiatives, his workers were becoming increasingly demotivated. When Eric approached them for ideas, their interpretation was that it was because *he* did not know what he was doing. Rather than gaining his employees' respect, Eric was starting to lose it.

He overheard conversations in the mailroom and cafeteria about how the previous boss "knew what he was doing" much more than Eric did. Eric's colleagues in other departments told him that the rumor was that he lacked confidence and decisiveness. He even heard through the grapevine that two of his star employees had already started to look around for other jobs.

After discussing the matter with some of his closest colleagues and friends both in India and the United States, Eric came to the conclusion that to be successful in India, he would have to adapt his behavior to the more hierarchical Indian leadership style. He would have to take that corner office, begin to make more unilateral decisions, and also start communicating with his employees in a more authoritative tone.

But he *really* didn't want to do that. He firmly believed that what he was doing was correct in terms of managing and leading people. And so he resented the fact that he would have to change to a *less* effective management style—from his perspective—in order to please his workers. It just didn't make any sense to him. Additionally, Eric dreaded the idea of having to act so far outside his personal comfort zone to manage in this new context. He had always hated working for authoritarian leaders in the United States, and the last thing that he wanted to do was to become one of these types of leaders himself. It felt disingenuous and unnatural. Finally, even if he were able to somehow convince himself to do it, Eric also had to admit that he was at a loss for how to actually be effective with this new kind of cultural style. Shedding this style felt like dropping his identity, and he didn't want to do that.

The combination of thoughts and feelings was overwhelming. All he wanted to do was to be effective, yet everything he was doing seemed to be backfiring. Eric had never failed on a management assignment, but he feared this might be the first time. That too made him anxious. As he sipped his cup of tea, Eric wondered if he had made a terrible career decision in moving to India.

A New Way of Understanding
Cultural Adaptation

If you have ever lived or worked in a foreign culture, you have likely confronted situations very similar to Eric's in which the natural, comfortable "default" behavior from your native culture turns out to be ineffective for a situation you find yourself in within a new cultural environment.

In each of these situations, you don't just struggle with *understanding* cultural differences. Rather, you struggle with the far more challenging task of actually *changing* your culturally ingrained behavior. I call this ability *global dexterity*—the capacity to adapt your behavior, when necessary, in a foreign cultural environment to accommodate new and different expectations that vary from those of your native cultural setting. For Eric Rivers, it's acting with a leadership style that fits his Indian setting and that differs from his own in the United States. Or for you, it's learning to adapt your behavior to function effectively in a particular situation in a foreign culture with expectations for behavior that are very different for how people would typically act in that same situation in your native culture.

Global dexterity is a critical skill for anyone from any culture attempting to function successfully in today's global environment. Business scholars and other writers have recently focused considerable attention on the importance of cultural knowledge, but being effective in a myriad of foreign cultural situations that you find yourself in when working or living abroad requires more than mere knowledge. It requires *the capacity to act on what you know*: the ability to mold and shape your behavior in foreign cultural settings so that you can be simultaneously effective and appropriate in that setting without losing who you are in the process.

Lack of Global Dexterity Can Limit Effectiveness

Global dexterity can be a challenging skill to acquire. You can feel anxious and embarrassed about your inability to master the new cultural rules; you can feel inauthentic when performing these new behaviors, especially if the new rules conflict with aspects of your ingrained values and beliefs. You can also feel frustrated and angry about having to adapt in the first place, wondering why the other side can't simply adapt to you. These feelings can interfere with your ability to successfully adapt your behavior—and, as a result, your professional reputation and effectiveness can suffer.

Here's an example. A few years ago I was speaking with an American manager at a company that had been recently purchased by a larger German firm. That manager was quite annoyed with his new German boss, whom he perceived as cold and uncaring. When I pressed him about why he had this impression, this manager said that the biggest problem was small talk. When they had first met, his German boss showed absolutely no interest in him as a person. He did not ask him any questions about his family—which was hard to do, given all the personal photos the manager had arranged on his desk and walls—and he also didn't comment on his interest in sports, which also was obvious from the many posters and photos on the wall. The boss simply came into his office, introduced himself, shook his hand quickly and coldly, and that was it. And this pattern continued into the future—no small talk, no effort to get to know him as a person.

I was curious about this story, so I followed up by interviewing several of the manager's German-born colleagues and asked for their perspective. It turned out that they knew about the importance of small talk in the United States, but felt uncomfortable doing it. In Germany, small talk is far less common than in the United States, and from a German perspective, it can feel superficial, irrelevant, and inefficient to engage in such random banter with a person you barely know. The problem, of course, was that in avoiding small talk, the executive inadvertently made a bad impression on his new employee and compromised his reputation within the firm.

The lack of global dexterity can also hurt your effectiveness at work. Take the case of Feng Li, a Chinese-born management consultant for a major American-based professional services firm in Chicago. I initially learned about Feng's case from Robert, one of the managing directors of the consultancy. Several years ago, Robert had hand-selected Feng to work for him in the managing director's office. Feng had impeccable oral and written English, outstanding technical skills, and was also very creative. He was on the fast track to senior consultant and then director, and eventually partner, except for one major issue: Feng could not get himself to participate actively in meetings. The problem had nothing to do with a lack of ideas.

Feng was one of the brightest consultants at the firm, and he had excellent ideas and insights. According to Robert, in terms of pure mental "firepower," Feng was at the top of the firm. The problem was that Feng was simply unwilling to contribute his ideas in a public forum.

Instead of raising his hand or his voice, Feng would remain silent in meetings. Nothing. Not a word. This was especially unusual given the culture of this particular firm, where, according to Robert, people typically had to bite their tongues not to speak and be noticed. Senior mentors would coach Feng, explaining that to get ahead, he would have to come at least halfway into the culture of the firm. They would encourage him to participate and contribute because they knew he had the chops. But Feng simply could not do it.

Robert himself tried to work with Feng to overcome these differences. He helped create a special role for Feng in these meetings, which would be an explicit role of authority—it would be Feng's job to own and drive the agenda within the meeting, and everyone would know that. Feng seemed to react positively to the idea, and Robert was encouraged. He was excited for Feng and also proud of himself for developing what really was a very clever idea. But it didn't work. Feng came to the meeting in this explicit facilitator role but remained silent, as he always did. Robert was tremendously frustrated. He wanted Feng to succeed, and the firm had spent a great deal of time and money trying to help him get ahead. But for some reason, he simply could not adapt to the culture. In the end, Feng ended up leaving the firm because of a "bad fit."

What You Will Learn in This Book

It's not easy to learn to adapt your behavior. And as we have seen, the stakes can be quite high. Failing to adapt successfully can have serious consequences—for people and for companies. But don't worry. This book will give you the tools to learn how to adapt your own behavior successfully in any situation you face and in any culture in which you operate.

The first lesson is that people can face three core challenges when learning to adapt their cultural behavior:

- The competence challenge: Feeling that your knowledge and skill is not up to the task of adapting behavior

- The authenticity challenge: Experiencing the new behavior as being in conflict with your accustomed way of behaving and with your preexisting cultural values and beliefs

- The resentment challenge: Feeling that the very act of adapting cultural behavior is a burden and an imposition.

Individually, any one of these challenges can be taxing, and collectively they can be very difficult to overcome. When you feel resentful about having to adapt behavior in the first place, embarrassed and anxious about your ability to do so, and awkward and uncomfortable about how disingenuous it feels to act so differently than you are used to, it's very hard to muster the psychological resources necessary to adapt your behavior.

So what can you do to overcome these challenges? How can you find a way of adapting behavior that does not feel so uncomfortable and inauthentic? It sounds impossible, but in fact, with the tools and frameworks that you will learn in this book, it's really quite straightforward. The key is to realize that you have much more power than you think to craft behavior that fits the new culture and that also fits you.

The first step is learning the new cultural rules, or what I refer to as the *cultural code*. Learning this code is key because it's the first step in helping you devise a way to feel authentic and be effective at the same time. It provides you with insight into the particular set of challenges you face when adapting your behavior in a particular situation and how you might be able to adjust your behavior in order to respond to these challenges.

What do I mean by the cultural code? You will learn that each situation you face—whether it's learning to give constructive criticism, make small talk, negotiate, participate at a meeting, or ask a favor of your boss—has certain rules for appropriate behavior in a given cultural setting (see "On Diagnosing the Cultural Code"). Although there are undoubtedly many different ways to characterize these rules, I portray them in terms of six dimensions that capture the expectations that others have for our behavior in a foreign setting:

- Directness: How straightforwardly am I expected to communicate in this situation?

- Enthusiasm: How much positive emotion and energy am I expected to show to others in this situation?

- Formality: How much deference and respect am I expected to demonstrate in this situation?

- Assertiveness: How strongly am I expected to express my voice in this situation?

- Self-promotion: How positively am I expected to speak about my skills and accomplishments in this situation?

- Personal disclosure: How much can I reveal about myself in this situation?

On Diagnosing the Cultural Code

As you read through the book, you'll notice that instead of providing you with the cultural code for every possible situation that you might face in a foreign culture, I instead provide you with a tool—the six-dimensional framework—that you can use to decipher the cultural code on your own.

Why not just provide you with an encyclopedia of all the cultural codes that you could possibly encounter, detailing, for example, how exactly you need to adapt your behavior to act effectively in China, India, France, and so on? Such a resource would certainly be useful and convenient. The problem is that it would be impossible to create—at least in a way that would provide you with practical information for the particular situation you're facing. That's because cultural codes are not generic. People often mistakenly assume that there is an "American" or "Chinese" or "Indian" code for behavior, and that once you understand this country code, you're set to interact successfully in any situation you encounter. But this is simply not true. Rather, these codes depend a great deal on so many other factors other than country-level differences.

Regional differences, for example, often matter a great deal—
such as the difference between the Midwest and Northeast of the
United States, southern and northern Italy, or the urban cities and
countryside of China. Company and industry cultures also greatly
affect the cultural code for the particular situation you face in
your work abroad. In China, for example, state-run enterprises
tend to have more "classically" Chinese cultural norms—empha-
sizing indirectness and modesty, for example, than Western- or
non-Chinese-owned companies. And of course, company norms
vary tremendously and make their own contribution to the cultural code for any particular situation. Finally, the preferences
and backgrounds of the particular people you interact with
may change the cultural code in your situation. You may be in
a culture that emphasizes assertiveness, but be interacting with
people who are quite atypical. As a thought experiment, imagine
trying to explain to someone how "directly" you are expected
to communicate in the United States. In very general terms, you
might say that communication norms in the United States are
quite direct, compared with many other cultures, but does that
hold in all cases? Would there be differences debating your case
at a vigorous brainstorming session with investment bankers in
downtown Manhattan, as opposed to a similar discussion with
more mild-mannered colleagues at a small bank in central Illinois?

The point is that cultural norms are not generic and that context matters a great deal. For that reason, it would be unadvis-
able to provide a list of cultural codes for you to simply slap on
to your own circumstances, because such a list would likely be
inaccurate and dangerously misleading, So, instead of a list, I

provide a flexible tool (detailed in chapter 3) that, with the help of knowledgeable colleagues and mentors, you can apply to any situation you may face in your work abroad to get a valid and reliable portrait of the local cultural norms.

Each situation you encounter in a foreign setting will have a specific cultural code for behavior along each of these dimensions. When motivating workers in India, there is a certain level or amount of assertiveness that you will be expected to show as a leader. When bonding with work colleagues after hours at a restaurant or bar in Japan, a certain level of enthusiasm is expected, which is quite different from how enthusiastically you are expected to behave in other situations that you might encounter in Japan.

I call the range of appropriate behavior along each of these dimensions the *zone of appropriateness*. When adapting our behavior across cultures, we often mistakenly believe that there is one very specific way of acting in that new setting—as if the required behavior were like the center of an archery target, and you received no "points" unless you hit that very specific bull's-eye. But that's simply not true. Instead, there is a zone—a range—of appropriate behavior, and your job is to find a place within this zone that feels natural and comfortable for you: somewhere within your *personal comfort zone*.

In an ideal world, this would be easy: your personal comfort zone would overlap nicely with the zone of appropriateness for behavior in the new culture and you could act appropriately and feel natural with little effort. Unfortunately, however, sometimes there is a gap rather than an overlap between the two—your personal comfort zone is quite distinct from the zone of appropriateness in the new culture. When attempting to act assertively with his Indian colleagues, Eric Rivers, for example, had a personal comfort zone that was well outside of the Indian zone of appropriateness, as illustrated in figure 1-1.

To become effective in this new setting, Eric had two options. The *unrealistic* option was to try to change the Indian zone of appropriateness; that is, somehow change the rules in India to fit with his existing preferences. The only realistic option was to *stretch* his personal comfort zone: to find a way of somehow becoming comfortable with a wider range of behavior than he typically was used to. By stretching his personal comfort zone, Eric could create an overlap between what was comfortable and natural to him and what was demanded in terms of effective and appropriate behavior in the new cultural setting (see figure 1-2).

FIGURE 1-1

Eric's original personal comfort zone

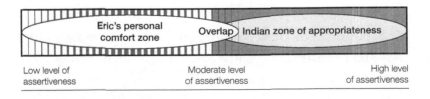

FIGURE 1-2

Eric's personal comfort zone after adaptation

In the pages ahead, you will have the opportunity to learn how to stretch your own personal comfort zone through a simple three-step process:

1. Diagnosis: Diagnosis means identifying the particular aspect of the new cultural behavior that is the most challenging in your particular situation. In Eric's case, it was assertiveness. Perhaps in another situation it might be directness or enthusiasm or personal disclosure. Using the six-dimensional approach highlighted above, you will learn how to diagnose the conflict you experience in any situation that you encounter and identify gaps between your personal comfort zone and the zone of appropriateness in the new culture.

2. Customization: Customization means putting your own personal spin on the behavior you need to show so that it feels natural to you and at the same time is appropriate and effective in the new setting. Customization also means creating your personal rationale for why you need to adapt your behavior in the first place. For example, instead of focusing on how the new behavior conflicts with your own values and beliefs, you might focus on how it is aligned with the cultural values and beliefs of the new cultural setting—and how natives in that setting actually expect you to act in this particular way, even if it feels awkward and unnatural to you. Customization is the answer to how you can have your cake (personal integrity) and eat it too (effectiveness).

3. Integration: Integration means becoming so familiar and comfortable with the new way of behaving that it becomes your "new normal": a way of acting

in a foreign setting that feels automatic and intuitive. Evaluation and feedback play a key role in this process. By periodically evaluating how you feel internally as you engage in the new behavior and also assessing your external effectiveness by gauging others' responses to your behavior, you can make ongoing adjustments in your style. The ultimate goal is to create a way of behaving that feels "just right"—natural for you and also effective and appropriate in the new setting. You will be surprised how easily this can be achieved with just a bit of strategy and effort and with the tools available to you in the rest of the book.

A few years ago I held a special forum in my MBA course in which senior managers from several different firms spoke with my students about the challenges of adapting cultural behavior. Each executive shared personal stories about the challenges that he or she had faced in managing and leading abroad and answered questions from the student audience. One particular moment stood out for me because it captured what I believe to be the essential challenge of developing global dexterity: an executive told us that the key to developing global dexterity was "to simply be yourself." Of course, this sounded quite odd to us. How can you adapt and at the same time remain who you are? The executive's answer was telling and has stuck with me to this day. He said that adaptation is indeed essential for success but that also, in his words, you have to make sure that you don't "bleach out who you are" in the process.

In this book I will provide a framework and set of tools to help you accomplish this objective: to build your global dexterity without losing who you are in the process. These tools will help you make sense of the challenges you face in adapting behavior abroad and to help you manage these challenges successfully. It will take some effort, although less than you might initially believe, and it might also take some courage. It's not easy to put aside what has worked for you for so long to adopt a completely different form of behavior. However, although challenging, this transformational experience can be tremendously rewarding—and in some cases, can even be fun. Let's dive in.

CHAPTER 2

Psychological Challenges of Developing Global Dexterity

Many people assume that knowledge is the key to intercultural success. But mere knowledge about cultural differences is not enough to be successful abroad. You need to be able to transfer that knowledge into action. From studying, observing, and working with hundreds of professionals over the past several years, I've discovered three core psychological challenges of adapting behavior across cultures:

- The authenticity challenge: The feeling that the new behavior is in conflict with your internalized system of cultural values and beliefs (which can create feelings of anxiety, distress, or even guilt)

- The competence challenge: The feeling that your knowledge and skill are not up to the task of successfully adapting cultural behavior (which can create feelings of anxiety, embarrassment, or even shame)

- The resentment challenge: The feeling that adapting cultural behavior is a burden and an imposition (which can create feelings of frustration or anger)[1]

You may not experience all of these challenges in a given situation, but you might. And chances are, at some point in your time abroad, you will.

The Authenticity Challenge: I Feel Disingenuous Performing Behavior That Conflicts with My Values

In some ways, adapting cultural behavior is like acting. To be effective on stage, actors need to master and then internalize a strange new script. So do individuals learning to adapt behavior across cultures, where they have to master and internalize new rules for culturally appropriate behavior. The big difference, however, is that in the world of theater, actors ultimately are not the characters they perform on stage—no matter how deeply they embrace their role. Their real self is separate from the character they are performing. They know that, and the audience does as well.

This is not the case for individuals learning to adapt their behavior in foreign cultures. When people switch to a different form of cultural behavior, they are not separate from the character they are performing, either in their own eyes or in the eyes of people observing them and drawing conclusions about them from their behavior. That is why people can experience such strong emotions when adapting behavior across cultures. They most often feel inauthentic behaving in a manner that feels unnatural to them and can feel doubly inauthentic knowing that others in the situation assume that this behavior is indeed a true reflection of who they are. The conundrum of developing global dexterity is that to be successful you have to adapt, but in the process of adapting, you can feel like you are losing yourself.

Delivering Negative Feedback in Germany

Consider, for example, the case of Larry Campbell, an American manager in Germany whose job was to manage a major organizational change project for one of Europe's largest tech companies. Larry was an excellent manager, and that's why he was chosen for this job. However, early in the process, he realized that his managerial style, which was very effective in the United States, was not translating so well into the German context. This was particularly apparent when he gave feedback to colleagues and subordinates—especially negative feedback. In the United States, Larry always prided himself on being able to deliver negative feedback in such a way that people got the message but did not get their feelings hurt. In Germany, this congenial style bombed.

Larry explained it to me this way: Imagine you are asking your colleagues what they think about an idea of yours. In the United States, the situation might unfold in the following way:

You: So, what do you think of the changes I made?

Your American colleague: I like them, but I'm wondering if our clients will understand what you mean by X,

Y, and Z. What if we thought about changing our approach?

The German version, on the other hand, would go something like this:

You: So, what do you think of the changes I made?

Your German colleague: They are wrong.

You: Oh—I see. What specifically don't you like?

Your German colleague: Our clients will not understand it. It will never work that way.

To most Americans, this feels overly blunt—to the point of being rude. But to most Germans, it is not rude at all: it's simply honest, and it's also precise and efficient. From a German perspective, there is no point in beating around the bush; if you have an opinion, you might as well state it, especially if you want to see improvement in the future. The problem for Larry was that in order to be accepted by Germans in this German context, he had to adapt his own behavior. He had to learn to be far more direct than he was used to. No protecting egos—just direct and "honest" criticism. And whenever he did it, Larry felt awful inside. It was completely against his nature to act in such a blunt manner. He felt overly aggressive—in his words, "like a hostile witness at a trial."

The difficulty that Larry experienced is certainly not unique. Even if someone like Larry has developed a careful understanding of the cultural rules in the new setting, he can still struggle inside because of how it *feels* to act in accordance with these rules.

Adopting an Authoritarian Style in India

This was certainly the case for Marco Boati, the forty-four-year-old Italian-born COO of a cutting-edge technology firm in Delhi. Having worked for many years in Europe and in the United States, Marco deeply believed in a participative style of management. By working together with employees to set goals and giving them the autonomy to achieve these goals and manage their own work processes, a manager could get far more out of employees than simply "telling them what to do." This style, however, didn't seem to work with his Indian subordinates, who would agree with Marco about project details but fail to execute them.

The problem came to a head when, during a critical effort at revamping the company's payment system to an all-electronic format, Marco's finance manager, Sandeep, failed to follow through on a series of critical assignments. Although Marco had shared the benefits of this change with Sandeep and there was a clear agreement to proceed with the new payment method, execution was lagging far behind. From observing how other Indian managers were motivating their subordinates, it became clear to Marco that he would have to change his style to be effective—a task easier said than done, as the new behavior that was acceptable within the Indian cultural setting conflicted with his deep professional and cultural values and felt awkward and uncomfortable to perform.

Marco recounted a case in which he felt as if he were literally berating the employee for failing to carry through with an assignment: "Sandeep, you have to do this! I told you three times already. You *have* to do it!" This time Sandeep listened to him and performed his required tasks. But although Marco had "succeeded" by acting in a way that was expected, appropriate, and acceptable in India, he felt guilty and distressed; he felt as though he was, in his own words, "scolding a young child."

Marco struggled in this situation because the behavior that he knew he had to adopt in order to act effectively in the new cultural setting was in deep conflict with his culturally ingrained values and beliefs. In this case, the conflict was around whether or not one should strongly criticize an employee in order to achieve management objectives. Every fiber in Marco's Western-trained mind was telling him one thing—that this type of behavior was unacceptable, even if it was effective and efficient for achieving his objectives. But his intellectual understanding of the Indian cultural norms was telling him something different: that he *had* to treat his employees in this way in order to be successful. The conflict between these two voices created such high levels of anxiety in Marco that he seriously wondered if he would ever be able to perform the behavior effectively.

Both Larry and Marco were certainly highly motivated to succeed. They knew how they needed to behave to act appropriately. They also had a thorough understanding of the cultural code in each setting, and of how the rules for appropriate behavior in their native culture were different from the rules for appropriate behavior in the new culture. What they struggled with was the conflict between these new cultural rules and their culturally ingrained values—about how to speak to a subordinate in Marco's case and how to deliver negative feedback to a colleague in Larry's.

Does that mean that people always experience identity conflict in every professional situation they encounter abroad? No—and in fact there were many situations that Larry and

Marco found quite easy to navigate in Germany and India. The point, however, is that in *these* key situations both Marco and Larry felt a strong sense of inauthenticity, and these feelings made it hard for them to be effective in their jobs.

The Competence Challenge: I'm Not Good at This, and People Can Tell

Imagine the following scenario: You're the CEO of a small high-technology start-up interviewing an applicant for an important new sales position in your firm. After weeks of wading through résumés, you finally find a candidate who seems perfect for the job.

"Hi! You must be Sergei!" you smile, as you walk over to the applicant and shake his hand.

"Yes," mumbles the man, as he weakly returns your handshake and proceeds to fix his gaze on the floor.

"Any problems finding the office, Sergei?" you ask, hoping to ease him into the interview with relaxed conversation.

"No," he replies, providing a perfectly accurate answer to your question, but at the same time disrupting your expectations for friendly conversation.

Undaunted, you try again. "So, Sergei, "Where do you come from? I mean originally?" you query in a folksy, friendly tone, hoping to draw him into "small-talk" mode.

"Moscow," he replies, yet again answering your question but disrupting your rhythm.

Frustrated by what you feel to be a clear lack of interest in friendly conversation, you realize you've made up your mind about Sergei. He's unfriendly, socially incompetent, and not a good prospect for your firm. Six months later, however, you are stunned to find out that Sergei has been hired by a competitor and is not only a reliable and efficient worker, but is also the leading producer at that firm. And you wonder what went wrong.[2]

What you might not have realized is that Sergei was indeed acting quite appropriately—for an interview in Russia. Whereas small talk is an essential part of American interviews, it is not at all part of the Russian script. In Russia, interviewers get right to the point, and any casual, lighthearted banter about topics such as the weather or the commute to the office is considered irrelevant and superficial. Eye contact and smiling are also not part of the script. In Russia, a job candidate does not make sustained eye contact with a potential superior: that would be considered rude and invasive in such a hierarchical society. Finally, the type of smiling considered appropriate in the United States would be considered overly familiar—and, frankly, foolish—in a Russian interviewing setting.[3]

Now imagine how Sergei may have been feeling as he was attempting to adapt his cultural behavior in this situation. Although it may not have been evident to you, it's very possible that Sergei was feeling quite anxious and even perhaps also embarrassed about his inability to navigate this new cultural routine. I actually know the Sergeis of the world quite well. As part of my PhD dissertation research, I followed many different foreign-born professionals from the former Soviet Union as they were attempting to switch their cultural behavior in the context of the American job interview. I was continually struck by how much these very accomplished professionals struggled, despite the extensive training that they had received about cultural differences.

The second challenge of developing global dexterity—the *competence challenge*—has to do with the struggles people encounter when they lack the knowledge and skills to function successfully in the foreign environment. This was true for Sergei and is also true for countless other people struggling to succeed abroad without a perfect mastery of the new cultural code.

Incompetence in the American MBA Classroom

Consider, for example, the case of Chang Han, a former accountant from Taiwan who was struggling to learn how to participate effectively in an American MBA classroom. Classroom dynamics are very different in the United States and Taiwan. In the United States, students are encouraged to participate actively and to debate and discuss with students and professors. In Taiwan, there is little, if any, open debate and discussion in class, and effective participation in the Taiwanese setting does not mean raising your hand. Instead, it means listening carefully and thoughtfully to a professor, taking notes, and reproducing this knowledge on a written exam.

You can imagine how Chang struggled adapting to the American system. Throughout the semester, Chang felt awkward and incompetent mastering these new cultural norms. He had a general sense of how he needed to behave—which, by his estimation, was more assertively and directly than his native Taiwanese style. But, he also never quite understood what "good" classroom participation actually meant. He certainly didn't want to appear too passive, but he also feared acting too aggressively.

The uncertainty was debilitating, and Chang felt ashamed and embarrassed at his lack of participation. He imagined that the professor thought of him as just another one of those "silent, invisible Asian students." He was self-conscious about making an acceptable comment and continually imagined what the other students in the class were thinking of him. Going to the professor and explaining the situation was a possibility. However, that too required a switch in behavior. Because of the strong hierarchical relationship between professors and students that Chang had internalized from his native cultural setting, Chang felt very uncomfortable approaching anyone about this predicament.

———————

Cultural researcher Geert Hofstede once wrote that culture is like software of the mind, and that depending on where we grow up, we each have a different form of mental software for making sense of the world and for guiding our actions.[4]

Adapting cultural behavior is like operating in a world requiring completely different mental software. Unlike actual software, which you can relatively easily "uninstall," our cultural software is deeply ingrained. That's what makes developing global dexterity so challenging and why it can make people feel anxious and incompetent. It's like being an actor preparing studiously for a role and then, on opening night, having everyone else on stage operating according to a completely different script.

Fumbling Around with Japanese Cultural Norms

That was certainly the case for Carla Green, who struggled early on in her job as a novice HR manager at a Japanese-owned company in New York City. Carla's first moment of true incompetence came during the first week, when a high-level Japanese executive walked into a junior staff meeting she was running. Carla was new to the company and to Japanese culture and had no idea how to respond. "Politeness," she thought to herself. "Just be polite." Luckily, she was not seated at the head of the conference table, because if she were, she knew that she would have had to get up and switch places, and that could be awkward. Instead, she was sitting at the center of the table facing the door. But as all this was going through her mind, something strange happened. Everyone in the room started looking at her! Why was she getting uncomfortable looks from her colleagues? Was she supposed to do something? And then it hit her. It wasn't the head of the table where the most important person typically sat in Japanese culture, as was the case in the United States. It was the center—and, in fact, it was her exact seat. Carla was mortified. She quickly got up to let the Japanese executive finally sit down and moved to a chair off in the corner and was silent for the rest of the meeting. That was her initial indoctrination to Japanese culture.[5]

That episode was only the first of many very uncomfortable moments for Carla at the Japanese firm. Learning this culture, she felt, was like writing with the wrong hand: it felt unnatural, and she was not good at it. Each time she had to make a decision about adapting her behavior, she felt a surge of anxiety: How was she supposed to act? What would people think?

One of the recurring challenges Carla faced was calibrating her behavior so that she would have just the right level of "indirect communication" with her boss. Carla knew that the ability to communicate information that is subtle but still gets the message across is a highly prized characteristic in Japanese culture, and was something she would have to learn to do in order to be successful at the firm. But it was very difficult for her to do, especially at first. Every time she started to speak more indirectly than she was accustomed to, she started to feel self-conscious. Was she being too indirect in that moment? Could her boss even understand what she was trying to say? Or was she being too direct, inadvertently offending him? Worst of all was the fact that she never got any feedback—or perhaps she did and wasn't able to decipher it correctly.

The Resentment Challenge: I Feel Bitter About Having to Adapt

In addition to feeling inauthentic and incompetent engaging in the new behavior, people can also experience considerable resentment over the fact that they have to adapt behavior in the first place. "Why do I have to adapt," they may wonder to themselves, especially in cases where the new behavior feels awkward, unnatural, or unnecessary. "Why can't the other person adapt to me?"

Doing Math Tricks to Succeed in Bangalore

That certainly was the case for Doug Jacobsen, an American finance professional in Bangalore, India, who was so bitter about cultural adaptation that he was on the verge of hopping on a plane back to the United States so he could live somewhere "normal" again. Doug had been in Bangalore for two weeks when he noticed a very strange phenomenon at work. Whenever people in his group were assessing a potential investment opportunity in a public forum, they would use what Doug came to call "mental math." They would start to work through the numbers associated with the deal—perhaps a $200 million market size, costs of $100 million, etc.—and they would add, subtract, multiply and divide these numbers right there in their heads and would proudly produce the results to the delight of the other members of the group. If the variables changed in the discussion—let's say that market size was $275 million and costs were $145 million, they would change their results on the fly as well. What frustrated Doug no end was that it seemed you had to be a human calculator to get anything accepted in this setting.

Doug was certainly no slouch. He was a top graduate of an Ivy League school, and had worked as a consultant for one of America's leading management consulting firms. He was smart, capable, insightful, and motivated. He just wasn't good at mental math. Doug realized that, at least in the short term, he would have to somehow learn to switch his cultural behavior to accommodate to this setting. However, inside he felt that it was totally ridiculous; and he felt deeply resentful of having to engage in what he perceived to be a completely unnecessary and irrelevant form of mental gymnastics.

This third cultural adaptation challenge—the resentment challenge—occurs when people experience the very act of adapting cultural behavior as being unfair, inequitable, or an imposition. Such individuals can feel considerable frustration, and even anger, about having to act in a manner so inconsistent with their culturally ingrained values and beliefs in order to be appropriate in a new cultural setting.

Having to "Sugarcoat" Performance Feedback

Another illustration of the resentment challenge comes from Marcus Thomas, an outgoing, charismatic, Caribbean-born associate at a large law firm in Houston, Texas. Marcus loved his job at the firm except for one glaring challenge: his inability to adapt to an American management style, especially when it came to delivering performance feedback to peers and subordinates.

In the Caribbean, as Marcus explained to me during one of our conversations, "You just tell it like it is. You don't sugarcoat feedback like in the United States." For example, when you make a mistake in soccer as a young child, your coach chastises you. He tells you that you did a terrible job and explains what you did wrong. The same goes in business. You don't protect a person's feelings when giving performance feedback. You just communicate the message and expect the employee to listen— and improve.

Not surprisingly, Marcus ran into trouble applying his style in the United States. He told me one story about how he was called into his partner's office the day after giving what he felt was straightforward and constructive performance feedback to one of his employees. The partner told Marcus that the employee was completely distraught after the conversation—she had gone home immediately and did not want to continue on the project. She even considered quitting her job. It was a huge mess.

Marcus was frustrated and angry. Why should he have to sugarcoat feedback to protect his employees' egos? And if someone had to adapt, why did it have to be him? Why couldn't his subordinates simply recognize that he had a different method—a stricter, more authoritarian style that happened to work quite well from where he came from? After all, he was the boss.

Three Separate Challenges Equals One Big Challenge

You can see how these three separate challenges can create one big problem for anyone learning to adapt behavior in a foreign setting. Feeling that the new behavior is in conflict with your culturally ingrained values and beliefs—the authenticity challenge—creates feelings of guilt and distress. Feeling that you don't do something well, and that this incompetence is visible to others—the competence challenge—creates feelings of anxiety and embarrassment. Feeling imposed upon to have to adapt in the first place—the resentment challenge—elicits frustration and anger.

The disruptive emotions that people experience from one, two, or all three of these challenges can interfere in a number of ways with developing global dexterity. In some cases, when the psychological toll is particularly intense, individuals will avoid adapting behavior altogether. In other cases, people do try to adapt, but the emotions "leak" into their performance. Marcus, for example, might praise the employee for a job well done, but not appear genuine when doing so. Larry might try to act with a German style of directness, but feel distracted inside by how uncomfortable it feels to engage in the behavior. When you avoid these challenging situations or handle them only at a sub-standard level, it impacts not only your internal state, but also your reputation and career advancement. It can also impact your organization.

Remember Eric Rivers, whom we met in chapter 1? Eric was losing the trust and respect of his Indian colleagues to such an extent that they were threatening to leave the firm. Marcus's rough style was so off-putting that it was demoralizing his employees, which had implications for the timeliness of a par-ticular project as well as for his and his employees' future with the firm. And for Marco, the Italian COO in India, frustrations about having to change his own personal style were carrying over to other parts of his work and home life.

So what can you do in order to be more effective at manag-ing yourself in these foreign cultural situations where success-ful adaptation is critical but also highly challenging to achieve? The answer, it turns out, requires a simple, but powerful reori-entation of your cultural mind-set. Rather than experiencing yourself as a prisoner of culture and cultural differences—as people often do when grappling with the difficulties of having to adapt behavior—you can instead come to realize that you actually have tremendous leeway to shape and craft your own foreign cultural experiences.

Now it's time to address how you can respond to these chal-lenges, which is the focus of the next section of the book.

Assess Your Own Level of Competence, Authenticity, and Resentment

Start by selecting a particular situation that you'd like to focus on. Examples might be "making small talk with my colleagues in New York" or "giving feedback to my supervisor in Berlin." It can be any specific situation that is challenging to you.

Name Your Situation

My situation is:

_____

_____

Next, answer the questions below and use the following scoring system to arrive at your answer.

Not at all			Somewhat			Very much so
1	2	3	4	5	6	7

Competence Self-Assessment

1. I am very good at performing this new cultural behavior. _____

2. This behavior is easy for me to perform. _____

3. I feel confident performing this behavior. _____

Add up the results for items 1–3. If your overall score is above 15, that indicates a high level of competence. Scores between 12–15 indicate a moderate level of competence. Scores below 12 indicate a low level of competence. If you score in this range, it means you could use additional practice and guidance in this situation.

Authenticity Self-Assessment

1. I feel like I'm doing something wrong
   when engaging in this behavior.   _____

2. This behavior feels really foreign to me.   _____

3. I do not feel genuine performing this behavior.   _____

Add the results for items 1-3. Overall scores above 15 indicate a low level of authenticity. In other words, you feel quite awkward, unnatural, and disingenuous performing the behavior required of you in this situation. Scores between 12-15 indicate a moderate level of authenticity. Scores below 12 indicate a high level of authenticity. These are among the easiest situations in a foreign culture because you can act appropriately and be yourself at the same time.

Resentment Self-Assessment

1. I feel that it's unfair that I have to
   accommodate my behavior.   _____

2. I feel resentful about having to change
   my style to fit theirs.   _____

3. I feel strongly that they should adapt to me;
   not the other way around.   _____

Add the results for items 1–3. Overall scores above 15 indicate a high level of resentment. Scores between 12–15 indicate a moderate level of resentment. Scores below 12 indicate a low level of resentment. These are situations where you adapt your behavior quite willingly.

PART TWO

How to Develop Your Own Global Dexterity

n this next section of the book, you will learn how to develop your own global dexterity with a simple three-step process.

- Step 1: Learning the rules for appropriate or effective behavior in the new setting and identifying the particular challenges that you will face when adapting to these requirements.

- Step 2: Learning how to customize or personalize your behavior so you can be appropriate and feel comfortable at the same time.

- Step 3: Integrating what you have learned into your personal repertoire through rehearsal and evaluation.

Ready to get started?

CHAPTER 3

Diagnose the New Cultural Code

You're in a foreign culture and want to be effective. But you also have a sense that the rules are quite different and you can't quite pinpoint what these differences are. The purpose of this chapter is to help you solve this problem.

Tej's Story

A former software engineer and manager for Citibank in Mumbai, Tej, as she likes to be called by her close American friends, brings strong technical skills, a cosmopolitan outlook, and an engaging personality to her job search in the United States. Passionate about pursuing a career in management consulting, Tej has all the strengths she needs to land a job but one: promoting herself at career fairs and at informal networking events. The process of getting a job in India relies much more on a person's concrete work and educational experience or on close personal contacts than on the informal networking that is so prevalent in the United States.

There are no "elevator speeches" in India. Job candidates are not expected to be as enthusiastic and assertive with a potential employer as they are in America—the process is far more formal, and candidates are expected to behave in a more deferential and restrained manner. Given these differences, it's not hard to understand why Tej feels so anxious, awkward, and embarrassed during networking conversations in the United States and fails in her initial attempts to find a job. Tej knows *how* to behave, but the difficulty of actually using this knowledge interferes with successful adaptation.

A Six-Dimensional Approach for Diagnosing the Cultural Code

The first step in developing global dexterity is learning a system for diagnosing the rules for behaving appropriately and effectively in a new cultural setting. Let's use Tej's example to see how the six-dimensional approach identified in the introduction of the book can help identify key differences between the two cultural styles.

These six dimensions represent key aspects of communication that differ across cultures, and that previous researchers in psychology and cross-cultural communication have shown to predict important personal and professional outcomes. Of course, there are many potential dimensions of communication style, and these six features are not the only dimensions that exist, or that differ across cultures. However, in my experience, this particular set does an excellent job at capturing cultural differences in a succinct, but comprehensive manner:

- Directness: How straightforwardly you're expected to communicate in a particular situation. Are you expected to say exactly what you want to say, or to "hint" at something in a more indirect manner?

- Enthusiasm: How much emotion and energy you are expected to show when communicating. Can you express how you feel, or is it more appropriate to hide your positive feelings?

- Formality: The amount of deference and respect you are expected to display with your communication style. Are you expected to show a high level of respect when com municating with someone in a particular situation, or can you be more informal?

- Assertiveness: How strongly you are expected or allowed to voice your opinion and advocate your point of view in a particular culture and in a particular situation in that culture. Should you be forthright in expressing yourself, or work at hiding or sublimating your point of view?

- Self-promotion: The extent to which you can speak positively about yourself in a given cultural situation. Should you actively promote your positive qualifications or be more self-effacing?

- Personal disclosure: The extent to which it is appropriate to reveal personal information about yourself to others. Should you be open and forward in expressing details about your life, or is it more appropriate to hide these personal details?

Communicating with a Potential Employer: India Versus the United States

Indian cultural norms differ quite significantly from American cultural norms along all six dimensions, as indicated in table 3-1.

People in India are expected to speak less directly about their accomplishments in a conversation with a potential employer and also normally do not outwardly express high levels of enthusiasm. In fact, American-style enthusiasm in such a situation would be seen as inappropriate—as exhibiting too much positive emotion for a serious, formal situation such as a job discussion. Indians are also accustomed to

TABLE 3-1

Cultural norms: India versus the United States

	India	United States
Directness	Low	High
Enthusiasm	Low	High
Assertiveness	Low	High
Self-promotion	Low	High
Formality	High	Low
Personal disclosure	Low	High

speaking quite formally and deferentially with a potential boss, at least as compared with Americans. Not surprisingly, assertiveness is also quite different in the two cultural settings: Indian employees are unlikely to speak with any degree of assertiveness toward a potential boss. Rather than acting in a strong, dominant manner, Indian employees are expected to show the reverse: a high level of deference and submissiveness toward a potential superior. This is quite the opposite from the American context, where too little assertiveness comes across as being meek and timid.

Self-promotion is yet another key area of difference between the two cultures. People in the United States are accustomed—even expected—to promote themselves at a networking event. It's a core aspect of the cultural code for that situation. In India, in contrast, people are not expected to speak openly about their accomplishments, and if they were forced to do so, would likely feel self-conscious and embarrassed. Finally, Indians are less likely to reveal personal information to a potential boss during a networking interaction; again, in contrast to Americans, who are trained to speak freely and easily about at least certain personal details during the small-talk portions of such discussions.

Given these differences, it's not surprising that Tej experienced so many challenges! However, cultural differences are not always so extreme: some situations will present challenges along only one or two dimensions of the cultural code. What the six-dimensional approach offers is a tool for helping you diagnose exactly where the source of the challenge that you face is so you can develop ways of resolving it.

Test-Driving the Six-Dimensional Approach: An American Manager Working in China

Tej's example showed how the six-dimensional approach can apply to the case of Indians networking in the United States. Let's now test-drive it in a very different context, imagining the situation of Michael Black, an American manager working in China for one of the country's biggest consumer products manufacturers. We'll see how the six-dimensional approach captures some of the key cultural challenges that Michael faces when managing in this new cultural context.

Situation 1: Michael Tries to Involve His Chinese Employees in Decision Making

After a quick cup of coffee and a brief glance at his e-mail messages, Michael calls in Wei, a member of his staff, to talk about a new project. Next week, Michael has a key meeting with his boss about the rollout of a new product. To prepare himself for that meeting, Michael wants Wei to prepare an analysis of competing products in the Asia-Pacific marketplace. Ever since arriving at the company, Michael has been quite impressed with Wei and believes that he is certainly capable of handling such an assignment. The conversation goes something like this:

> *Michael:* I have a meeting next week with my boss to discuss design strategy for this new product. And I'm thinking that an analysis of competitor products should be helpful. What do you think?

Wei: I think that's a good idea. So what kind of information are you looking to see?

Michael: Anything that you feel is relevant is good to have. Use your best judgment on what to cover.

Wei: Okay.

ANALYSIS

In many ways, this conversation is unremarkable. It's happening in Beijing, but it could just as easily happen in Brussels or Boston. Moreover, the behavior is also relatively unremarkable from the perspective of Western or North American cultural norms. A boss, Michael, is discussing the parameters of a key work task with his subordinate, Wei—and is even encouraging Wei's input into the decision-making process.

Unfortunately, however, as you may have already anticipated, this Western cultural style of involvement—treating a subordinate as almost an equal in the decision-making process—runs counter to the more assertive, hierarchical expectations for the boss in the Chinese cultural code. From that perspective, Michael is not acting assertively enough.

No Chinese boss has ever told Wei to "use his best judgment" or do what he feels is "relevant." Chinese bosses typically communicate with a much higher degree of assertiveness with their employees. With this in mind, you can now imagine how Wei's question, "What kind of information are you looking to see?" was a sort of plea for more direction and assertiveness from Michael. From Wei's perspective, taking personal initiative is risky. He might end up disappointing his boss by taking the project in an unexpected direction or, worse, might disrespect him by drawing a conclusion that conflicts with Michael's point of view.

Situation 2: Michael Tries to Promote Himself for a Special Assignment

After meeting with Wei, Michael takes the elevator up to the finance division to visit Xiaodong Liu, a human resources manager in charge of selecting participants for a prestigious leadership development program in Singapore. Ever since he arrived at the company, Michael had heard about this program and has been anxious to participate. Michael has had numerous interactions with Xiaodong and feels comfortable approaching him about this. He walks over to Xiaodong's office and knocks on the door.

> *Michael:* Hi, Xiaodong! How're things? Do you have a minute?
>
> *Xiaodong:* Sure, Michael, come on in. Please have a seat.
>
> *Michael:* Thanks. I heard you're looking for people to participate in the Singapore leadership development program. I'd love to be a part of this team.
>
> *Xiaodong:* Hmmm. I think you'll be a good fit.
>
> *Michael:* I'm really glad you think so. I actually think I'd be a great fit, given my background and skill set.

ANALYSIS

Once again, from an American perspective, this behavior is unremarkable. To be sure, Michael is enthusiastic and self-promoting, but in the corporate circles he's familiar with in the United States, he needs to act this way to be heard—after all, only the squeaky wheel gets the grease. Again, however, this behavior is inconsistent with the Chinese cultural code's expectations for levels of self-promotion, directness, and enthusiasm. Rather than overtly advertising himself as a "great fit" for the position, a more culturally sensitive version of Michael might have instead hinted at an interest in the program in a far more indirect manner. For example, he might have noted the number of years that he had been with the company, perhaps even commenting on the leadership training program as an "interesting opportunity." The goal would be to let Xiaodong connect the dots about his interest and then, if he feels it appropriate, invite Michael to participate.

Situation 3: Michael Tries to Assert Himself During a Business Discussion

Following his meeting with Xiaodong, Michael meets with one last colleague, Tong Liu, about a research project that the company is conducting to develop a sense of consumers' preferences in the Asian market, and how these preferences might be changing in the next five to ten years. This project is requiring lots of collaboration across different divisions of the company and Michael needs to talk with Tong about some staffing issues. He walks into Tong's office and sits down with Tong and three of Tong's subordinates:

Tong [presenting his plan to Michael]: So, that's the plan for this project. We'll need four people, ten hours a week . . .

Michael [interrupting Tong]: Four people ten hours a week? No, I think you're too optimistic. With the level of thoroughness we're looking to achieve, there's no way we get this done in time with four people.

Tong: Well, that's just a rough estimate for now. Of course, we can adjust the number when the scope of the project is more clearly defined.

ANALYSIS

As I'm sure you have guessed, Michael has committed another faux pas in confronting Tong in such an assertive and direct manner, especially in front of his subordinates. From Michael's perspective, he probably was just being "honest" and a "straight-shooter"—which, to him, felt genuine. But from a Chinese perspective, it is face-threatening to be told *no* with such bluntness in a group setting. It disrupts the harmony of the group, which is so crucial to Chinese social interaction.

If Michael were to have switched to a more Chinese-oriented approach, he might have hinted at his displeasure, instead of expressing it so directly, saying something like "Hmm. We'll have to think about that," or "That might be possible" instead of the overt "No," which likely rubbed Tong the wrong way.

How You Can Diagnose the Cultural Code

When you think about the cultural code, you probably immediately think of *national* cultural differences—how China is different from Canada, how India is different from France, how England is different from Germany, and so on. And you're right: national cultural differences do matter. The way you network in India indeed does tend to be different from how you network in the United States. The way you motivate employees in Japan is quite different from how you do so in Canada.

The mistake isn't thinking that national cultural differences matter. The mistake is thinking that they are *all* that matters. It turns out that many other factors matter in addition to national culture when determining the cultural code, including company or industry norms, regional norms, and individual differences in the backgrounds and experiences of the people you are working with, as indicated in figure 3-1.[1]

For you to diagnose the cultural code in a given situation that you are experiencing in a foreign culture, the key is to ask yourself a series of simple questions (also see "You Can Be a Cultural Detective"). Although you might not know all of the answers immediately, you will probably be surprised at what you do know, and also at what you can quickly find out with a small bit of research.

FIGURE 3-1

Factors that shape the cultural code

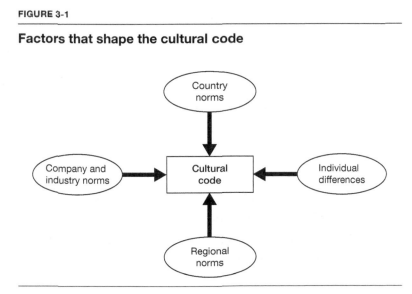

You Can Be a Cultural Detective

You don't need an encyclopedia to diagnose the cultural code of a country, region, organization, or even work group. All you need are your own powers of observation and deduction. Although it can certainly help to have lived in a culture for a long time or to speak with someone familiar with the culture, you can also quickly capture the code's essence by asking yourself a series of simple diagnostic questions, using the six dimensions of the cultural code. For example:

- Directness: Do people tend to be succinct in what they say and get right to the point—often with as few words as possible—or do they tend use broader, more general, or ambiguous language, often hinting at what they mean without saying it directly?

- Enthusiasm: When something positive has happened, do people tend to express their feelings openly, through facial expressions, body language, and tone of voice or do they tend to hide or suppress the outward expression of positive feelings, despite what they might feel inside?

- Formality: Do people tend to dress conservatively, make official appointments to speak with each other, and use titles such as "General Manager" or "Doctor," or are they more likely to dress casually, informally knock on each other's doors to have a chat, and refer to each other by first names or even nicknames?

- Assertiveness: Do people tend to express their viewpoints strongly and forcefully and without hesitation (such as "We definitely need to do this") or do they express opinions in a more tentative and cautious manner (such as "I think maybe we should consider doing this")?

- Self-promotion: Do people tend to highlight, exaggerate, or draw attention to their personal accomplishments or do they tend to minimize, underplay, or qualify what they have achieved?

- Personal disclosure: Do people keep conversations strictly about business, or do they also discuss details of their personal lives with colleagues at work?

What Do You Know About the Country?

The first question to ask yourself is what can you learn—or what do you already know—about the *country* where this situation takes place? One important national cultural difference to consider, for example, is directness of speech. In certain cultures, people tend to communicate with what Westerners might refer to as a very indirect style of communication. For example, in a meeting in Japan, a Japanese executive would rarely if ever directly say "no" to a proposal, instead communicating his displeasure through much subtler means. Cultures like Japan, China, and Korea are often referred to as *high-context* cultures because listeners in these cultures depend on a detailed understanding of subtle verbal and nonverbal cues within the immediate context to make sense of communications. In contrast, the United States, Australia, and Israel are *low-context* cultures, where communication is more explicit and less dependent on these subtle nonverbal cues. Although not every person from a high- or low-context culture will necessarily operate with the culture's characteristic style, knowing whether you are in a high- or low-context culture will let you make an educated guess about the likely cultural code for the situation you're in.[2]

For example, imagine the following situation. You are a British manager working in India with a team of local Indian subordinates. Of all the members of your team, you respect your product manager Deepa the most because of her extensive knowledge and intuition about the Indian marketplace. You set up a meeting with her to talk about a new idea you have for a product launch and the conversation goes something like this:

You: So, Deepa, what do you think about this new product idea? Have you had a chance to look at the materials?

Deepa: Yes, I have.

You: What do you think?

Deepa: I like it. It looks like there's a lot of competition, and you've done a very thorough job in outlining all the different competing products.

You: I wanted to understand all the different market segments and where we might fit in. But what do you think of the product idea itself? Do you like it?

Deepa (hesitates): I do. I remember you also had another idea a few weeks ago. Is that also integrated into this proposal?

You: No—I had more or less decided against that, but I'm keen on this new idea. Do you think it's something we can go with?

Deepa: When you say "go with," do you mean launch immediately?

To a Western ear, Deepa might sound a bit passive and perhaps also slightly cautious, asking a lot of different questions about the boss's idea and never quite answering him directly or joining in his enthusiasm. From an Indian point of view, however, Deepa's message is quite a bit stronger: she's essentially saying that she does not like the new product idea and that it would be a mistake to launch it. Does she ever actually come out and say that? No, she doesn't, and such indirectness would be characteristic of the Indian culture, where direct criticism of a boss's idea could be seen as disrespectful and potentially face-threatening to the boss as well.[3]

In addition to understanding a culture's level of directness or indirectness when diagnosing the cultural code, it is also useful to know whether you are in a high- or low-power-distance culture. *Power distance* refers to the extent to which power is equally distributed within a society and how people communicate with each other up and down the organizational hierarchy. In high-power-distance societies, such as China, Korea, Mexico, and Malaysia, hierarchical communication norms are very strong, and people in these cultures tend to speak quite formally and deferentially to people in higher power positions. In contrast, in low-power-distance societies, such as Denmark, Sweden, Israel, and the Netherlands, people are less hierarchically organized and also less apt to show high levels of deference and formality to authority figures.[4] Again, although not every person from such a society will reflect these power distance norms, being aware of the general societal norms of the culture you are interacting in is good practice for gauging the cultural code for your particular situation.[5]

What Do You Know About the Region?

Just as it is useful to learn something about the norms of the culture when diagnosing your situation, it is also good practice to learn something about the norms of the region. Consider the case of a Japanese manager, Hideki, who was sent to the United States by his Japanese automotive company to express anger with suppliers who had continually failed to deliver key parts on a timely basis. Although I've noted that Japanese are often hesitant to express emotion in business situations, it turns out that the supplier/client relationship is quite distinct in the culture, and clients are often given considerable latitude to express emotion when dissatisfied with the service relationship. So it was Hideki's task to express this dissatisfaction and, by doing so, fast-track supplies for a key product launch.

His plan was to come on quite strong and express his dissatisfaction in a very forceful manner. He knew that the American culture was relatively direct and he also assumed, from a similar experience in New York, that it would work in any American market. What he failed to realize was that the small town in Iowa where he delivered this latest message was quite different from New York. In fact, he was caught completely off-guard: the friendly Midwestern managers at the factory in Iowa were shocked by Hideki's candor and vitriol. Reading this on his counterparts' faces, he quickly tried to soften his approach, but the damage was done. The relationship became very difficult to repair and was a burden for Hideki going forward. Had he altered his approach to fit this different regional culture, this unfortunate outcome might have been avoided.

What Do You Know About the Company or Industry?

You are diagnosing the cultural code for a situation you're facing in a foreign culture and you've considered the country and regional norms; but how about the company or industry? Like countries and regions, companies and industries also have distinctive cultures. How you interact with your boss at Google is quite different from how you interact with your boss at Microsoft or Intel. Meetings at traditional, bureaucratic organizations are often run quite differently from meetings at small start-ups. Norms for behavior in the advertising industry are quite different from norms for behavior in the agricultural industry and so on.

Of course, sometimes the culture of a company is not so distinct and can actually be quite similar to the culture of a region or a country. For example, a traditional Saudi steel company in Riyadh may very likely have norms that are traditionally Saudi, such as a relatively high level of power distance. In contrast, imagine the cultural norms of a global consulting firm like McKinsey that also happens to be in Riyadh. Because the consulting firm is a global organization with norms influenced both by the local culture and by its Western "DNA," chances are that the firm would have norms that are actually slightly divergent from the Saudi norm.

What Do You Know About the People?

When diagnosing the cultural code of a situation you encounter in a foreign culture, ask yourself what you know, or what you might be able to find out, about the people you are interacting with. Are you communicating with a sixty-year-old senior executive or a twenty-something manager? People who are older are often more likely to reflect the norms of the overall society. It would also be useful to know if the people you are interacting with are *locals*—born and raised in that particular setting and without extensive travel experience, or if they are *cosmopolitans*, with extensive travel background. Locals are much more likely to reflect the norms of the immediate region you are in, whereas cosmopolitans are likely to be open to a wider range of potential behaviors.

Finally, the particular role that you are playing in a given interaction matters a great deal as well. For example, many East Asian and Southeast Asian cultures, such as India, China, and Korea, have relatively indirect norms of communication, especially from a subordinate to a superior, whereas superiors in these cultures are often quite direct with their subordinates. It's therefore critical to understand the role that you play in a given situation in order to properly diagnose the appropriate cultural style.

Diagnose the Cultural Code for a Situation of Your Own

Now it's time to apply the ideas presented in this chapter to help diagnose the cultural rules in a situation of your choosing. Start by selecting one situation that you find challenging because of the cultural differences it presents. Examples might be "providing feedback to my boss in Tokyo" or "motivating my team in Shanghai."

Name Your Situation

My situation is:

_____

_____

The next step is to begin assessing the cultural code for your situation. You are actually going to assess two different codes: the cultural code of the new culture and the cultural code of your native culture. For each dimension of the cultural code, circle what you believe to be the range of expected behavior in your native culture and in the new culture. By examining these in tandem, you will be able to see quite clearly the areas of potential conflict between the two codes for your situation.

You may find it challenging to diagnose the cultural code for your situation if you are unfamiliar with the culture to begin with. This can be a great opportunity for you to seek help from a colleague who is familiar with the new culture and who can help you diagnose the code. You never know: the person you choose to help you with this exercise might end up becoming a valuable cross-cultural mentor to you. Once you are ready, you can complete the following assessment:

(1) Directness

How directly am I supposed to communicate *in this particular situation*? Am I expected to say exactly what I want to say, or am I expected to hint at what I want to say in a more indirect manner?

Level of expected directness: In my *native* culture

Low level			Moderate level			High level
1	2	3	4	5	6	7

Level of expected directness: In the *new* culture

Low level			Moderate level			High level
1	2	3	4	5	6	7

(2) Enthusiasm

With how much enthusiasm am I expected to act *in this particular situation*? Am I expected to act in an excited manner, showing a high level of positive emotion, or am I expected to act in more neutral, subdued manner, hiding emotions rather than expressing them?

Level of expected enthusiasm: In my *native* culture

Low level			Moderate level		High level	
1	2	3	4	5	6	7

Level of expected enthusiasm: In the *new* culture

Low level			Moderate level		High level	
1	2	3	4	5	6	7

(3) Formality

With how much formality am I expected to behave *in this particular situation*? Am I expected to act in a formal, proper manner, or in a more casual, informal, relaxed manner?

Level of expected formality: In my *native* culture

Low level			Moderate level		High level	
1	2	3	4	5	6	7

Level of expected formality: In the *new* culture

Low level			Moderate level		High level	
1	2	3	4	5	6	7

(4) Assertiveness

With how much assertiveness am I expected to act *in this particular situation*? Am I expected to act in a strong, dominant, manner in this situation or in a more passive, submissive manner?

Level of expected assertiveness: In my *native* culture

Low level			Moderate level			High level
1	2	3	4	5	6	7

Level of expected assertiveness: In the *new* culture

Low level			Moderate level			High level
1	2	3	4	5	6	7

(5) Self-promotion

Am I expected to speak positively about myself and my accomplishments *in this particular situation*? Or am I expected to hide or understate these aspects of myself?

Level of expected self-promotion: In my *native* culture

Low level			Moderate level			High level
1	2	3	4	5	6	7

Level of expected self-promotion: In the *new* culture

Low level		Moderate level			High level	
1	2	3	4	5	6	7

(6) Personal disclosure

Am I expected to share personal information about myself *in this particular situation*? Or am I expected to share little about myself?

Level of personal disclosure: In my *native* culture

Low level		Moderate level			High level	
1	2	3	4	5	6	7

Level of personal disclosure: In the *new* culture

Low level		Moderate level			High level	
1	2	3	4	5	6	7

CHAPTER 4

Identify Your Own Challenges with the New Cultural Code

So, you've diagnosed the new cultural code for a particular situation you face in the new culture, or at least you have an informed, educated guess. It's now time to diagnose which aspect of the code causes you the greatest degree of difficulty. To do this, you have two diagnostic tools at your disposal: the *zone of appropriateness* and the *personal comfort zone*.

The Zone of Appropriateness

The *zone of appropriateness* captures the range of behavior that is acceptable and appropriate to natives of a new culture. As someone learning to switch cultural behavior, your goal is to get your behavior inside this zone because that's where you will be seen as appropriate and effective.

As an example, let's go back to Tej's story from chapter 3 and take a look at self-promotion within the context of an informal networking event in India and the United States. In the United States, informal networking is self-promotional by nature. Employers expect candidates to promote themselves and their accomplishments, albeit with a certain degree of modesty. Thus, one might imagine that the zone of appropriateness for the networking event in the United States falls somewhere in the 5 to 6 range on a 7-point scale.

As has been noted, the norms for self-promotion in India are very different. Indians are more deferential and modest in such situations, and thus the zone of appropriateness in India would be on the other side of the scale—say, a 2 or a 3.

Your Personal Comfort Zone

Understanding the zone of appropriateness in a new culture is a critical first step toward developing your global dexterity. Equally important, however, is assessing the fit between the new culture's rules for appropriate behavior and what feels natural and comfortable to you. To do this, you need to locate what I call your *personal comfort zone*. Whereas the zone of appropriateness captures how others in the culture you're operating in assess their cultural rules, the personal comfort zone captures your own level of ease with these rules.

What determines our personal comfort zones? Most of us are products of the cultures we were raised in, in the sense that we embody to some extent the core values and beliefs of our native culture. But this is not always the case. In some cases, our own personal styles do not necessarily match the prototypical style of our native cultures.

Imagine, for example, the case of Yang Wu, a Chinese-born consultant working for a professional services firm in the Netherlands. At this particular firm, the organizational culture is highly participative. All consultants, no matter their level, are expected to actively contribute to group discussions. Unfortunately, this norm is difficult for many of the East Asian consultants at the firm who are not used to such active participation, especially in front of senior colleagues and partners.

Imagine that Yang, however, has had a very different experience from his East Asian colleagues. His father was an executive for a Chinese business when Yang was young and as a result, Yang has traveled and lived extensively overseas. He spent his high school years at an international school in Paris, where he was exposed to a more Western system of education. Yang considers himself Chinese to the core, but is also quite comfortable with other modes of interaction. As a result, unlike many of his Chinese colleagues who struggle with active participation and debate, Yang enjoys it. He does not need to adapt his behavior to be successful in these situations. Instead, he can just be on autopilot and act according to his default behavior—which, luckily for him, is in complete congruence with the cultural ideal of the firm.

Unlike Eric Rivers from chapter 1, Yang is lucky because his personal comfort zone fits that of the new culture. What's critical to look at is the degree of overlap between your personal comfort zone and the zone of appropriateness for behavior in the new cultural setting.

Linking the Two: The Zone of Optimal Performance

Linking the zone of appropriateness and your personal comfort zone can help you identify gaps and overlaps between what's appropriate in the new setting and how you feel comfortable behaving. Let's return to Tej's example. As figure 4-1 suggests, Tej's personal comfort zone is quite distinct from the American zone of appropriateness when it comes to self-promotion. As a result, Tej struggled at promoting herself in the United States, feeling inauthentic and anxious acting in a manner that was so far removed from the range of behavior she felt most comfortable performing.

Of course not all people from the same culture are alike, and so, for someone with a different personal comfort zone, the circumstances could be quite different. Imagine, for example, that Tej has an Indian colleague, Raj, whose personal comfort zone for self-promotion is much wider than Tej's. In fact, his personal comfort zone actually *overlaps* considerably with the American zone of appropriateness, creating what we can call a *zone of optimal performance*, where Raj can be himself and at the same time act appropriately (see figure 4-2).

FIGURE 4-1

Tej's personal comfort zone versus the American zone of appropriateness

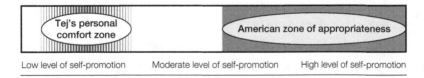

Low level of self-promotion   Moderate level of self-promotion   High level of self-promotion

FIGURE 4-2

Raj's personal comfort zone versus the American zone of appropriateness

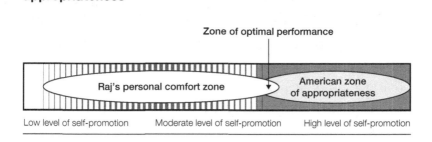

Why do Tej and Raj have two different personal comfort zones? It could be because Raj is more outgoing by nature; or perhaps he has more experience in the American culture and has adopted certain aspects of this new cultural code. In any event, because of the overlap, adaptation for Raj is quite straightforward: to be effective, all he has to do is be himself—albeit a certain version of himself that overlaps with the American expectation.

Let's look at another example. Curtis Jones is an American executive working for a Japanese company based in New York City. Curtis's challenge is delivering feedback to his Japanese employees, who are used to a far less direct style of feedback than Curtis is accustomed to giving. Curtis explained it to me this way: If a subordinate in the United States delivered a contract to him that was full of errors, he would likely say, quite straightforwardly, "You made a mistake" or "You need to redo this because it is wrong." With Japanese employees, however, he has to communicate the message much more indirectly.

When Curtis first worked with Japanese employees, he felt quite uncomfortable communicating so indirectly because, from his American cultural perspective, it felt imprecise, disingenuous, and also risky: what if the person didn't actually get the message? Over time, Curtis has learned to stretch his personal comfort zone and feel quite at home in the Japanese zone of appropriateness, as indicated in figure 4-3.

Instead of having to say "This is wrong" or "You made a mistake," Curtis might now get the same message across in an indirect (and harmony-preserving) manner; for example, "As you know, accuracy of these reports is very important. Please review this again just to double-check that it's absolutely correct and to insure that we do not send incorrect information."

A very different example comes from Xin Wong, a Chinese marketing analyst for a major consumer products company in the United States whose challenging cross-cultural situation is learning to promote herself at work in order to attract the attention of senior managers. In China, you simply do your work well and are recognized and rewarded for your

FIGURE 4-3

Curtis's new personal comfort zone

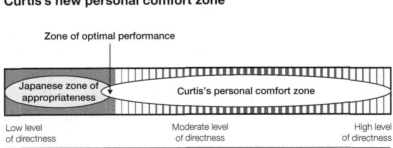

accomplishments. Drawing attention to this work—even in a subtle way—would be perceived as immodest and inappropriate. Yet, in the United States, Xin knows that she must to learn to self-promote to be recognized for her accomplishments and advance in her career. As you can see from figure 4-4, the gap between the expected level of self-promotion in the United States and that in China is very wide.

Unfortunately for Xin, her personal comfort zone for self-promotion is quite narrow and there is no overlap at all between her comfort zone with self-promotion and the American zone of appropriateness. Rather than a cultural *overlap*, this is a cultural *gap*. This cultural gap creates quite a bit of distress for Xin, who must struggle to adapt successfully.

She needs to self-promote to develop her reputation at the firm and be placed on career-advancing projects. But what she actually has to do and say in order to promote herself feels uncomfortable and unnatural. Does this mean that there is no possibility of her ever succeeding in this situation? No, of course not. However, it does mean that the challenge is steep and that it will take skill and strategy to bridge the gap—this will be the topic of chapter 5.

FIGURE 4-4

Xin's personal comfort zone versus the American zone of appropriateness

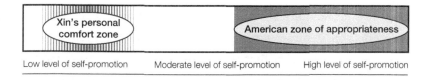

| Low level of self-promotion | Moderate level of self-promotion | High level of self-promotion |

Identify the Particular Challenges You Face with the New Cultural Code

Now it's time to apply the ideas presented in this chapter to help you identify the particular challenges you face adapting to the new cultural code. Start by selecting a situation that you find challenging because of the cultural differences it presents. This might be the same situation you focused on earlier or a completely new one.

Name Your Situation

My situation is:

_____

_____

Assess Your Personal Comfort Zone

The next step is to assess where within the new culture's code of behavior you feel most comfortable. Do you have a wide personal comfort zone? Or is your personal comfort zone much narrower—that is, do you feel comfortable only with a very specific level of, say, directness or enthusiasm?

For example, imagine that you are an American learning to give performance feedback to your boss in Tokyo. Assume that you have completed this exercise, and that figure 4-5 captures your personal comfort zone with respect to "directness."

Figure 4-5 suggests that you have a relatively wide personal comfort zone in this area: you are comfortable behaving with a

FIGURE 4-5

Your personal comfort zone for directness

Directness

high level of directness and also with a moderate level of directness. However, you are not comfortable acting with a low level
of directness in this situation—unfortunate for you, because as
we will learn shortly, that's exactly the style of behavior that is
demanded of you in the Japanese cultural setting.

Now, draw your personal comfort zone for each element of the
cultural code for your chosen situation by circling the range of
behavior that you would be comfortable with.

It may help you to think about the level of anxiety you experience
along a spectrum in your personal comfort zone. Right in middle
is where you should experience no anxiety at all. You may experience a bit of anxiety along the far edges of your zone in either
direction, but not much. If the anxiety is enough to be a problem,
you are likely outside the zone of personal comfort.

(1) Directness

Low level		Moderate level			High level	
1	2	3	4	5	6	7

(2) Enthusiasm

Low level			Moderate level			High level
1	2	3	4	5	6	7

(3) Formality

Low level			Moderate level			High level
1	2	3	4	5	6	7

(4) Assertiveness

Low level			Moderate level			High level
1	2	3	4	5	6	7

(5) Self-promotion

Low level			Moderate level			High level
1	2	3	4	5	6	7

(6) Personal disclosure

Low level			Moderate level			High level
1	2	3	4	5	6	7

Identify Gaps and Overlaps

You have diagnosed the code and identified your own personal comfort zone. Now you can put these pieces together to identify gaps and overlaps between the new code and what is natural and comfortable to you.

Let's continue with the previous example of giving feedback to your boss in Tokyo: on the right side of figure 4-6 is your personal comfort zone from before; on the left is the zone of appropriateness for this behavior in Japan. In this case, there is no overlap between your personal comfort zone and zone of appropriateness. So you would likely struggle with adapting your behavior in this situation—at least at first.

Let's now shift the example and imagine that there *is* an overlap between your personal comfort zone and the zone of appropriateness in the new culture, as illustrated by the interlocking ovals in figure 4-7.

FIGURE 4-6

Your personal comfort zone versus the Japanese zone of appropriateness

Directness

FIGURE 4-7

Overlap between your personal comfort zone and zone of appropriateness

Directness

In this example there is an overlap between your personal comfort zone and the zone of appropriateness. As a result, you can act comfortably and appropriately at the same time in this situation.

It's now your turn to assess the gaps and overlaps that you experience for each dimension of the cultural code for a situation that you have chosen to focus on. As a first step, draw an oval representing your personal comfort zone for each dimension of the cultural code. Next, draw a second oval representing the zone of appropriateness for that same dimension. Notice for each dimension whether there is a gap or an overlap.

(1) Directness

Low level			Moderate level			High level
1	2	3	4	5	6	7

(2) Enthusiasm

Low level			Moderate level			High level
1	2	3	4	5	6	7

(3) Formality

Low level			Moderate level			High level
1	2	3	4	5	6	7

(4) Assertiveness

Low level			Moderate level			High level
1	2	3	4	5	6	7

(5) Self-promotion

Low level			Moderate level			High level	
1	2	3	4	5	6	7

(6) Personal disclosure

Low level			Moderate level			High level	
1	2	3	4	5	6	7

CHAPTER 5

Overcome Challenges by Customizing Your Cultural Behavior

You have learned how to diagnose the new cultural code and to determine the challenges that you will likely face when accommodating to this code: in other words, where you experience gaps between how you would comfortably and naturally behave (your personal comfort zone) and how you need to behave to be effective and appropriate in the new cultural setting (the zone of appropriateness). The next step is to work on solutions—to devise a way of overcoming these challenges.

The first step in this process is to learn how to customize your behavior. Customizing behavior is a bit like purchasing a suit and having it tailored to your exact specifications. You take it off the rack, wear it a bit so you can see how it works

for you, and then bring it to a tailor to make it fit just right—
letting it out a bit here, taking it in a bit there. Like wearing
a customized piece of clothing, adapting cultural behavior
does not mean having to stuff yourself into a garment if it isn't
exactly your style. The tailoring changes the garment, but it's
still something you chose; it still allows you to express your own
individuality. Just as you can customize clothing, you can also
learn to customize your cultural behavior using the following
customization tactics described below.

Make Small, but Personally Meaningful Adjustments

How can you customize your behavior to make it both acceptable to others and also acceptable to you at the same time? Your
tendency may be to think big—to think of major changes in
how you behave. However, what I find most successful is actually to think *small*—to make small, but meaningful adjustments in how you act so that you infuse part of yourself into
the behavior while maintaining cultural appropriateness (see
table 5-1).

TABLE 5-1

Customize your behavior

Make yourself feel more natural by making small, but personally meaningful
adjustments in:

➢ What you say

➢ How you say it

Putting a Russian Spin on American-Style Assertiveness

Let's look at the case of Irina Pavlova, a management consultant from Russia working for a major US consulting company. Irina's cultural adaptation challenge was learning to be assertive in asking her boss to place her on high-profile projects at work. At the particular firm where Irina worked, there was a quarterly internal competition to decide which consultants would be placed on the most compelling projects. Placement on these projects was an opportunity to build skills and generate visibility within the firm—both of which were critical for promotion. In fact, when she first arrived at the firm, Irina watched with amazement at how others vigorously advocated for themselves, saying that they'd "love" to "take on" a particular project and that they'd be the perfect person for the job.

It made Irina sick to think about how important this behavior was, and also how uncomfortable it would be for her to perform it. Irina came from a culture where vying for projects and, more importantly, speaking assertively with one's boss was simply not part of the cultural fabric. So, for Irina, this behavior was particularly challenging along the assertiveness dimension of the cultural code. There existed a significant gap between her own personal comfort zone and the zone of appropriateness in the US culture—or at least in the culture of her particular firm. She struggled with this challenge for months, knowing what she needed to do, but afraid that in adapting behavior she would lose herself in the process.

Eventually, Irina was able to make a very slight, but meaningful adjustment in her behavior that had a significant impact on her experience. Instead of using direct, assertive language like her colleagues (e.g., "I'd love to take on that project"), Irina chose to phrase the statement in the form of a question—*asking if she could be helpful* in taking the lead on a particular project. She phrased the request as a question, but the overall message was that she was actually vying for the position—and in fact, she would then follow up by explaining why she would be a good choice. However, by leading with a question instead of a statement, Irina reduced her discomfort and found a way to be effective and authentic at the same time. It felt more deferential, polite, and just more her style.

Putting a Greek Spin on Meetings in Luxembourg

Minor linguistic changes such as those adopted by Irina can actually have a relatively major effect on people's experiences of the new cultural norms. That was definitely the case for Kostas Papadopoulos, a Greek banker learning to adapt his behavior during business meetings in Luxembourg. In Greece, meetings were, as Kostas put it, a "complete free-for-all." People wouldn't think twice about expressing their opinions loudly and assertively, even if someone else was speaking. And Kostas liked it that way. He loved the Greek culture—it was in his blood and felt alive to him. That's why it was so hard to adapt to Luxembourg's controlled, methodical, orderly business culture. He felt like a fish out of water.

Initially, Kostas tried his natural Greek style, but he quickly learned from the dismayed looks on his colleagues' faces how inappropriate this behavior was. He wanted to accommodate and be effective, but he also did not want to lose himself in the process. His solution? Like Irina, he made a minor, but meaningful accommodation. Rather than aggressively inserting his voice and point of view into a discussion, as he would have done in Greece, Kostas used polite expressions as a tool for softening any interruptions he would make. He would say things like "Sorry for interrupting" or "If I may," and then glance at the relevant person to make sure it seemed OK to continue speaking. In Greece, these niceties would be unnecessary—and in fact, he might have even been perceived as "weak" if he had used them. In Luxembourg, however, they helped him create a blend between an important aspect of his personal style that he did not want to relinquish and the more civil Luxembourg culture.

Putting an American Spin on a Chinese Interview

A very different example of customizing comes from David Carry, an American manager looking to relocate to China after several years' work experience in the financial services industry. David's cultural struggle concerned Chinese interviewing norms, which are very different than those with which he was most familiar. In China, unlike in the United States, the emphasis in interviewing is on fitting in and being part of the system. Yet David did not see himself—or want to present himself—as someone who could merely fit in. Quite individualistic by nature, David had always seen himself as unique, and able to provide unique value. He didn't want to just be a cog in the machine. He wanted to shine. However, this attitude did not work in China, as David realized after a slew of unsuccessful job interviews.

Eventually, after much trial and error, David hit on a solution that represented a relatively small accommodation, but one that was successful both internally for him as well as externally. What David did was to create a blend between individualism and collectivism. He accommodated to the Chinese standard to show that he was sincere in adapting to that culture. However, he also retained part of himself in the process by peppering the basic Chinese script with occasional references to his uniqueness and how he could provide the firm with unique value. In the end, this blend was successful, as David himself noted: "I was more individualistic than what would be expected from a Chinese interviewee, but I was sure not to show too much individualism. That would make me come across as ignorant of the cultural norms and expectations."

Blending Israeli and American Feedback Styles

Anat Berger, an Israeli consultant working for a professional services firm in the United States, is another example of a professional who used customization as a strategy for fitting in without feeling disingenuous. After only a few months on the job, Anat was surprised to learn that her cultural style of giving frank, demanding feedback was intimidating fellow workers and giving her a negative reputation in the firm. In Israel, Anat had always been taught to deliver straightforward feedback. After all, what is the purpose of giving feedback unless you communicate directly and honestly? However, in the United States, as Anat quickly learned, people were used to a much softer style. An Israeli colleague of hers referred to this style as the *sandwich approach*: the negative part of the message is "sandwiched" between positive feedback at the beginning and end. It's a way to cushion the blow and protect a person's ego when delivering potentially negative news.

Yet this approach felt disingenuous to Anat, and every time she used it in practice sessions, she felt evasive and as if she were obscuring the truth. She considered multiple ways to resolve this conflict but in the end found an effective way to customize her style. Rather than use the full sandwich approach, Anat decided to use an "open-faced" sandwich, giving only one dose of positive feedback at the beginning rather than sandwiching the feedback between two doses of praise. In this way, Anat was able to retain her "Israeli edge" but also accommodate to US expectations for appropriateness. Her colleagues' comments confirmed this view. They felt that her behavior was far less intimidating than before. It was clearly more direct than the typical American style, but was appropriate and effective. Most importantly, it was something Anat could work with. It was a way of accommodating her behavior without losing herself in the process.

Personalizing a PowerPoint Presentation

A final example of customization comes from John Drake, an American manager working at a US industrial firm that had recently been purchased by a much larger German company. John was a true entrepreneur. If you gave him a task, John would figure out a way to get it done—his way, and it would almost always be in a way that worked better than you had imagined.

A problem arose, however, when John's spontaneous, impro-visational style conflicted with the strict focus on protocol at the German firm. John respected the efficiency and productivity of the German style, but it also felt constraining. In the old organi-zation, all that mattered was that the work got done. Under the new German owners, on the other hand, it sometimes felt as if the process was even more important than the end result. All the checklists, check-ins, standard protocols, and other procedures felt overly bureaucratic—and, frankly, like a waste of time.

Ever the entrepreneur, however, John came up with a plan to inject a bit of himself into his work in the new culture. He knew that he could never make major changes to the standard protocol because it was so central to the new culture. However, he realized that he did have some leeway to customize his experience—and that's exactly what he did.

One day, while delivering a PowerPoint presentation to the group, John did something no one at the firm had ever done. The presentation was about communicating a new organiza-tional change process to employees across the globe, and John was making the point that unless the communication was novel and memorable, there would be negative consequences.

What type of consequences? John clicked to the next slide, which his colleagues undoubtedly expected to be an excel graph, but which instead was a photo of his kids sleeping on a hammock. The American colleagues in the room laughed; the German colleagues also smiled. It was a bit risky, but John fig-ured that if he couldn't inject a bit of himself into the process, he wasn't staying at the company for the long term anyway.

Luckily, the photo was a hit, in part because it was genuinely funny, but also because the rest of his presentation was on point and had followed firm protocol. This was an example where injecting even a bit of his true self helped John find a way to feel authentic and get the job done.

Customize How You *Think* About the New Behavior

In addition to changing your behavior, you can also ease cultural adaptation by making meaningful adjustments in how you interpret and make sense of a behavior you need to adopt. You can develop your own story for why this new behavior is acceptable for you to perform. Just as no two behavioral adjustments are alike, no two stories are alike. Using the tools of psychological customization, you will find ways that make sense for giving yourself *psychological permission* to engage in this new behavior and, in doing so, reducing the inner conflict that you experience.

Irina's Story

Irina Pavlova's heart was racing. She took a deep breath, got up from her office chair, and walked down the hall to her boss's office. This was it. This time she was really going to do it. For days she had been putting off this important conversation.

The problem was that she kept getting passed up for important assignments. Irina wished that her boss or her boss's boss would notice her excellent qualifications and assign her to these career-building projects—just like in Russia. But she knew that this was unlikely. Eventually, Irina realized that in addition to adjusting her behavior itself as we saw earlier, she also needed to find a way to give herself psychological permission to act more assertively. This meant finding a way to feel that it was indeed okay for her to act in a manner that at least initially she experienced as being in conflict with her cultural values and beliefs. She had to somehow find a way to legitimize in her own mind the idea of actively promoting herself.

Most people living or working in foreign cultures experience some version of this dilemma. They know that in order to succeed, they have to adapt. But by adapting, they feel as though they are giving up who they are and what they value. It can feel like an impossible bind, and many people are unwilling or unable to give themselves permission to engage in the behavior.

What I have found, however, is that when people like Irina put their minds to it, they are able to find a way to feel legitimate and comfortable. The key is to craft a personalized explanation that fits naturally with their values, beliefs, and personal goals. For some people, this explanation might focus on seeing adaptation as a means to achieve a goal that they really cherish. For others, learning to see the new behavior from the perspective of the new culture, rather than exclusively from their own cultural perspective, might do the trick. Still others will find a combination of different explanations and rationales that work. The key is to find a rationale that feels truly genuine and legitimate.

With that in mind, let me offer a menu of some different options that have worked for people I have studied and worked with throughout the years (see table 5-2).

TABLE 5-2
_____

Customize your perceptions

Make the behavior feel more acceptable to do by:

➤ Connecting it to your personal goals

➤ Connecting it to your personal values

➤ Connecting it to your cultural values

➤ Embracing the new culture's logic
_____

Link the New Behavior to Your Personal Goals

Although people are clearly performing new cultural behavior for a purpose, they often do not think about it—or at least aren't necessarily focused on it as they engage in the activity. Yet, thinking about this purpose can be quite motivational, especially if it is connected in some way to meaningful personal goals. Focusing on a worthy goal can give you the psychological permission to behave in a way that feels inconsistent with your cultural ideals. You may certainly still experience some discomfort, but it's is tempered by the fact that you are doing it for a purpose—and for a purpose that really means something to you.

You may recall Marco Boati, whom we met in chapter 2. The Italian-born COO of a cutting-edge technology firm in Delhi, Marco was deeply committed to succeeding as a manager in India. Part of the reason that he went there in the first place was for the challenge of learning to function effectively in a foreign setting. Reminding himself of that served as an antidote for the discomfort he felt when, in his words, he felt like he was "acting like Gordon Gecko"—speaking in what he felt to be an overly strong, assertive manner to his subordinates in India.

Another case is Jae Won Kim, the Korean-born CEO of a software company who encountered a cultural divide when opening a branch of his company in China. Jae Won was, in his own words, a "traditional Korean leader"—very strict, hierarchical, and tough with his employees. Moving into another Asian market, Jae Won naturally adopted this same authoritarian approach with his new Chinese subordinates, reprimanding his workers for the smallest technical error or deviation from protocol.

To his great surprise, however, his style, though "Asian," did not work. Used to a somewhat gentler and more paternalistic style, his Chinese subordinates became very anxious around Jae Won, even starting to avoid coming to work altogether. Jae Won quickly realized he had to adapt his leadership style for the Chinese context. But it felt strange and inappropriate to be so lenient with employees when doing so would be uncommon—and most likely ineffective—in Korea. Yet the more Jae Won was able to focus on the reasons that he was making this switch—for the sake of his business—the more he was able to see the behavior as a necessary evil that he was willing to perform for the greater good of the company.

Link the New Behavior to Your Personal Values

Cultural values are critical in determining how we behave and how we experience ourselves behaving in particular situations. What we often forget about, however, is that it is not only cultural values that matter in guiding and shaping our experiences—it's our *personal* values as well. These values are shaped in part by culture, but also by such things as our personalities, how we were raised, and our personal and professional experiences. In some cases, personal values are consistent with cultural values, but in other cases they are not.

Let's take Irina Pavlova as an example. Irina was born and raised in Russia, a culture that strongly values hierarchy and maintaining a significant power distance between those who are older and more experienced and those who are younger and less experienced. This is something reflected in many aspects of the society—in how parents treat children, teachers interact with students, and bosses interact with workers. This culturally ingrained value was also deeply ingrained in Irina and accounted in large part for the challenges that she faced in adapting behavior to the US setting.

However, at the same time that Irina's cultural values influenced her, so too did her personal values. For example, Irina deeply valued personal achievement. This strong personal value was instilled by her parents, who had lived under Communist rule and who felt that the only way for Irina to escape Russia's still-difficult economic and social conditions was through education and individual achievement. These strong personal values brought Irina into a yearlong abroad program at an American university during college, then to a prestigious US-based MBA program, and ultimately to a desirable position with a major professional services firm.

When I spoke with Irina early on, during her initial struggles at the firm, it was clear that she was experiencing the idea of acting assertively with her boss through the lens of her *cultural* values, and viewed through this Russian lens, the behavior felt very uncomfortable. Over time, however, Irina realized that her cultural values did not have to dominate her experience. If she could see what she was doing through her *personal* values—through the part of her that valued individual achievement through hard work—adaptation would become a far easier exercise. For example, instead of seeing her own assertive behavior through a Russian cultural lens—and feeling inauthentic and guilty as a result, she started to see the idea of vying for a prized assignment through the lens of her personal values—in particular, as being resonant with her strong values surrounding personal achievement. She also started to view the entire enterprise of learning to adapt behavior as a "task" that takes "hard work"—and viewed through the lens of "hard work," the experience of adapting behavior felt consistent with her personal work ethic. By shifting her focus from cultural to personal values, Irina was able to achieve a sense of authenticity engaging in behavior that initially felt quite inauthentic and uncomfortable.

Link the New Behavior to Your Cultural Values

On the face of it, this technique sounds counterintuitive. Don't the situations you need to adapt to conflict with your cultural values? Isn't that why they are so difficult? How can you reduce internal conflict by linking the behavior that runs counter to your cultural values to those very values?

What people sometimes overlook, however, is that they don't just have one cultural value—they have *many* cultural values. And while behavior may be inconsistent with one such value, it doesn't necessarily conflict with *all* of them. In fact, it's quite possible that the same behavior that is in conflict with the cultural value they find difficult is congruent with others. Recognizing these latent or hidden sources of cultural congruence can be a powerful tool in your arsenal for responding to identity conflict.

Let me illustrate with Tej, the Indian technology professional we first met in chapter 3. Remember how anxious, awkward, and embarrassed Tej felt when promoting herself in networking interactions in the United States? That was because she was making sense of the situation through one particular cultural value—the value of *modesty*. Viewed through this lens, self-promotion was in conflict with her Indian upbringing and very uncomfortable to do. As a result, she felt guilty and embarrassed.

What Tej did not realize, at least initially, was that the modesty lens was only one potential way for her to perceive this behavior. A very different way to view what she had to do was through the lens of *deference*—another of her deeply held cultural values. Through a modesty lens, the behavior felt inappropriate. But through a deference lens, the behavior felt more acceptable. If her object was to be deferential to potential employers, Tej had to accommodate her behavior to their expectations, which meant following American cultural norms. If not, it could make *them* feel awkward, which was the last thing she wanted to do. So simply by shifting her focus from modesty to deference, Tej was able to alter her experience.

Embrace the New Culture's Logic

Often, when we enter a new culture, we feel caught between two worlds. On the public stage, we are acting according to that new culture's rules. But on the inside, we still have our own cultural logic. We see and interpret the new behavior we are asked to perform according to our native cultural values, beliefs, and routines. When viewed through this frame, new behavior often feels very unnatural and can even feel inappropriate. My last piece of advice for customizing your perceptions around cultural adaptation is quite simple: *embrace the new culture's logic*. Don't just change how you *behave*: change how you *think*. Learn how and why the new behavior you're performing is appropriate in that culture's system; once you do, chances are the conflict will dissipate.

For example, Marco Boati came to see how the highly assertive style that he had to adopt to be effective in India was part of the Indian cultural fabric. As a result, he started to feel more acceptable adopting a stronger and more top-down leadership approach than he was used to in America.

Irina Pavlova came to appreciate how demonstrating interest and initiative to your boss and asking to be put on assignments was what was typical and expected in the United States, even though it was quite inconsistent with the Russian cultural paradigm. Once she was able to appreciate this distinction, putting herself forward became more a more palatable behavior.

The same was true for Curtis Jones, the executive working for a Japanese firm in the United States (see chapter 4). Curtis initially felt annoyed about having to adopt an indirect communication style, but once he really came to understand the Japanese perspective on the behavior—how critically important a person's public image and reputation are in Japan, and how damaging it can be to threaten a person's "face" with direct negative, public feedback—Curtis started to feel more comfortable with how he had to perform.

In all three cases, knowledge was the key to reducing cultural conflict. Once each person had come to a deep understanding of the new cultural rules, it became much more comfortable to perform the behavior.

————————

In sum, by customizing how you think about the behavior you are performing, you can reduce your feelings of discomfort. You can feel more authentic because the behavior feels more legitimate to perform, and you can also feel less resentful, because you are more enthusiastic about acting in a manner that makes sense to you and that does not feel like an unwanted imposition.

YOUR TURN

Customize Your Own Behavior

Name Your Situation

Choose a situation for yourself that you would like to work on customizing and describe it in the box provided below.

SAMPLE VERSION:

My situation is: Communicating negative feedback to an employee in Germany

This situation is challenging for me because: I have to act more directly and assertively than I ever would in the United States and each time I do it, I worry my colleagues and subordinates will think I am being unnecessarily harsh.

YOUR VERSION:

My situation is:

_____

_____

This situation is challenging for me because:

_____

_____

Adapting Your Own Behavior

One of the best ways of making your new behavior feel more natural and comfortable is to make it your own—to put your own personal spin on the behavior so that it feels authentic to you, but also still within the new culture's zone of appropriateness. Can you think of specific ways that you might customize how you perform the new behavior? These don't need to be major changes. In fact, the changes that Irina, Kostas, David, Anat, and John made in this chapter were quite subtle. However, in each case, they were able to put their own touch on the behavior and as a result make it their own.

SAMPLE VERSION:

*To cope with feeling unnecessarily harsh when deliver-
ing German-style feedback, I add short phrases like "I have
thought a lot about this" or "I have carefully considered this*

issue" before delivering the feedback. This lets the other per-son know that although I'm being quite direct and succinct, I have thought carefully about what I'm saying. It's not exactly how the typical German manager would communicate, but it works for me, and still seems to be effective and appropriate in the culture.

YOUR VERSION:

_____

_____

Customize How You Make Sense of the New Behavior

You can also make the new behavior feel more comfortable by changing your perceptions: how you think about the behavior you need to adopt. Try out the following tools with the situation that you have chosen to work on.

Strategy #1: Link the New Behavior to Your Personal Goals.

Why are you learning these behaviors? What is the goal of learning this new behavior? Is the goal to learn more about a new culture? Is it to be effective at your job? Is it to add value to your company? Is it to progress in your career? Is it something else entirely?

SAMPLE VERSION:

I am learning this behavior so I can be more effective as an expat manager in Germany and add value for my company.

YOUR VERSION:

_____

_____

How much do you care about achieving this goal? Why do you care about achieving this goal? Why is it important to you?

SAMPLE VERSION:

This goal is important to me because success in this German setting will enable me to be transferred to other overseas assignments, which will help me progress in the company. Succeeding in this assignment will also help me achieve my own personal goal of becoming an experienced global manager.

YOUR VERSION:

_____

_____

Strategy #2: Link the New Behavior to Your Personal Values.

Think about the range of your personal values. These are things that you care about and that motivate you. It might be that you are highly achievement oriented and strongly value personal achievement. It might be that you are very motivated to build meaningful friendships. Think of all these different personal values and try to think of at least two different ways that you might be able to see the new behavior as being linked to each of these values.

SAMPLE VERSION:

Learning to adapt my behavior in this situation in Germany
is linked to two of my personal values. First, it's linked to
my value of always wanting to learn and improve my skills.
Adapting my behavior in Germany is also linked to my per-
sonal value of respect—in this case, respect for the system of
behavior in a different culture.

YOUR VERSION:

_____

_____

Strategy #3: Link the New Behavior to Your Cultural Values.

Initially the new behavior you're performing might feel inconsistent with your cultural values. However, what people often forget is that they have many different values—not just one. Is there
any way that you can see this behavior, which is inconsistent
with certain cultural values, to actually be consistent with other
cultural values? Examples of values might include such things as:
achievement, deference, modesty, self-advancement, humility,
individualism, collectivism, or a group orientation.

SAMPLE VERSION:

I see performing this new behavior as being linked to my cul-
tural values of achievement and individualism. Achievement is
something I strongly value, and something that I see as being
a strong value of the United States. Adapting behavior in this

setting will help me be more successful at my job. Individual-
ism is also another strong American value, and by putting my
own personal spin on the new behavior, I can feel like I am
not just fitting in with the crowd, but doing something that is
effective and appropriate, and at the same time true to who I
am as a person.

YOUR VERSION:

_____

_____

**Strategy #4: See the Behavior from the Perspective of the
Other Culture.**

Imagine that you need to explain to someone from a different
culture about why people in *your* culture act as they do in the
situation you're focusing on. How would you explain this cultural
logic?

SAMPLE VERSION:

Although it's hard to generalize about how people provide
negative feedback in every situation and context in the United
States, most people tend to soften negative feedback with
some element of positive feedback, often before and some-
times even after delivering the negative feedback. The pur-
pose is to soften the blow and protect the ego of the person
receiving the negative message.

YOUR VERSION:

_____

_____

Now you are going to do the same thing for the new culture. How would you explain the cultural logic for why people behave as they do in this situation in the new culture? What do you think are the key differences between the two cultural logics or rationales for behavior?

SAMPLE VERSION:

It seems from talking with Germans and from working in Germany for some time that Germans in this situation value precision and honesty over protecting a person's ego. That's why they tend to deliver feedback in a manner that is more direct and straightforward than in the United States and also tend not to focus as much on protecting the ego of the person receiving the message.

YOUR VERSION:

_____

_____

CHAPTER 6

Integrate What You Have Learned Through Rehearsal and Evaluation

You've mastered the new cultural code. You've learned which aspects of adapting to a new culture are most challenging for you and why this is the case. You've even started to work on these challenges by adjusting your behavior so that it feels more legitimate and acceptable. What's next?

The next step is to make these initial changes stick: to make them feel like they are second nature; to develop a comfort level with actually using this behavior in real situations. In sports, people use the term *muscle memory* to describe the way a movement or action that initially requires analysis and concentration becomes instinctive through practice and repetition. The muscles themselves develop a "memory" for the activity so that it is performed automatically and unconsciously.

The goal here is to achieve the same level of fluency for your new cultural behavior, and to do that requires a system of rehearsal. Thus, the next step in the customization process is to find ways to rehearse what you have learned—ideally in a context that exposes you to performance pressure without the full level of stress of the ultimate performance environment.

Samuel's Story

Imagine the following situation: Samuel Mohammed is a Nigerian-born consultant working for a US-based consulting firm in Chicago. Although his technical performance is excellent, Samuel has been told at his last performance evaluation that, unless he starts actively participating in brainstorming discussions at the firm, his chances for promotion will be limited. But Samuel does not like participating in these meetings. In fact, he dreads it. Born and raised in a very hierarchical Nigerian culture, Samuel is deeply uncomfortable with the thought of participating, especially with people with more seniority and experience. When he was a child, it was deeply instilled in Samuel to "speak when spoken to" and that children are "to be seen and not heard." This was true at home, at school, at the university, and then ultimately in his initial working experiences at Africa.

Not surprisingly, Samuel's first performance review was deeply disappointing. He thought he was doing an outstanding job—after all, his technical work was excellent, and he had become the informal "go-to" person for solving complex problems at the firm. However, Samuel was so reticent in meetings that many in the firm—especially those in senior leadership positions—knew little about him, just that he was polite and quiet and a good technician.

Samuel was frustrated that this aspect of his cultural background was such a liability. But he also was highly motivated to succeed. So, Samuel did what any good consultant would do: he created a *performance improvement plan*. The goal of the plan was to improve his ability to participate more successfully at meetings.

Rehearsing Cultural Behavior—in Three Acts

For anyone learning to adopt an unfamiliar, even uncomfortable, cultural behavior, rehearsal serves a critical function in the cultural adaptation sequence. It enables people to "try on" new behaviors and see how it feels to use them in a realistic situation. It also enables them to *take their internal pulse*—to see how it feels on the inside to act in a manner that feels in conflict with their personal or cultural values and beliefs and to develop ways of reducing this internal tension.

In theater, rehearsal often takes place in a three-step sequence. Actors initially become familiar with their roles by reading the script and getting a feel for the characters they will be playing. Next, they experiment with their roles and adjust how they perform them in simulated practice sessions with others on stage—the rehearsal. Finally, the actors perform in front of a live audience during a practice run—the dress rehearsal. These three stages of familiarization, basic rehearsal, and dress rehearsal enable actors to learn about, customize, and eventually internalize the role that they are called upon to perform.

Learning to act in a foreign culture is very similar, and the people we have met in this book have engaged in the same type of process. Using Samuel's example, let's take a closer look at each of these stages and how you might adapt your own cultural learning to this three-stage process.

Act 1: Familiarization

The first stage is the *familiarization stage*, where you try on the new behaviors to see how they fit and feel. This is similar to going to a department store to try on a new suit or a new pair of shoes. You put on the shoes or the suit, look in the mirror, walk around, see how it feels, how it looks. That's just what you're doing when initially learning the new cultural behavior: familiarizing yourself to see if—and how—these new behaviors can become part of your personal repertoire.

In Samuel's case, familiarization entailed observing colleagues, learning from his boss, and then participating in some simple role-play exercises with his roommates to get a feel for the new behaviors. In other cases, people might decide to practice with colleagues in a very informal setting, or even rehearse by themselves in front of the mirror or on videotape.

Act 2: Rehearsal

After familiarization comes the *rehearsal stage*, where you really start to explore what it is going to be like to use these behaviors in a real situation. During this stage, you are doing more than getting a feel for the role you will play. You are actually playing that role on stage—albeit in a simulated situation without an actual audience to judge you. Samuel was creative in finding a unique opportunity to rehearse his new behaviors.

Samuel had kept in close contact with colleagues who had started with him as junior consultants and who were still with the firm, albeit now in different divisions and doing very different work. Now, every Tuesday, he and four or five members of this cohort had an informal lunchtime get-together at a local Chinese restaurant. Typically, the conversations at these lunches were very casual, and topics spanned the gamut from work to television to sports to relationships. But for this particular lunch, Samuel asked his colleagues if they could take a few minutes to simulate a brainstorming session, with each of his friends playing a different role in the meeting. Of course, it was not entirely realistic, as Samuel and his friends were gobbling up Chinese food, and the conversation only went on for a few minutes. However, because his colleagues were familiar with the company and could simulate actual situations, the conversation was far more realistic than the ones he had with his roommates, who knew nothing of the work the firm did.

Also, because his colleagues were familiar with the context, they could provide some useful feedback to Samuel about how he was participating in the discussion. For example, Samuel learned that in certain cases, behavior he felt was too assertive was actually not assertive enough in his colleagues' eyes. In other cases, behavior that Samuel felt was just about right in terms of assertiveness and directness was actually judged by his colleagues as being too aggressive.

This basic rehearsal stage provides an excellent opportunity to practice fledgling skills in a setting with elements of realism, but without the high stakes and pressure of an actual performance situation. For example, at various times in his rehearsal, Samuel was able to "hit the pause button" and start over, or stop the session to get quick feedback on whether his colleagues thought his approach was working.

Act 3: Dress Rehearsal

You have crafted and customized your role. You know how you need to behave and have even practiced it a few times in a rehearsal situation. It's now time to put what you have learned into action.

But before you do this in a real-world situation with real stakes and consequences, it is useful to practice in a realistic, but slightly less consequential situation that we might call a *dress rehearsal*. Dress rehearsal is different from regular rehearsal because the performance is conducted as if it were opening night. It occurs before a live audience and does not include stops, starts, or pauses in the action. However, dress rehearsal is also still practice. For that reason, it is useful to use real situations for dress rehearsal, but situations that are less consequential versions of the ultimate situation you are preparing for.

Samuel used an interesting venue for his dress rehearsal. He was on the board of directors of a small nonprofit organization, and the board met on a monthly basis to discuss strategy and fundraising. Typically in this setting—as at work—Samuel was reluctant to speak up, primarily because the other board members were far more senior and experienced than he was.

This time, however, Samuel decided to go for it and speak his mind: he recognized that it was an excellent opportunity for him to practice and hone his new skills. It was realistic enough for him to have the experience of brainstorming in a professional setting, but safe enough to practice because the situation did not have the same stakes as the brainstorming discussions with his senior colleagues at work. Having done this successfully, Samuel felt better prepared to put these behaviors into use at his next meeting.

To truly experience and learn to manage the psychological challenges of adapting behavior, it is critical to practice in a realistic environment and ideally, at first, in one where the stakes are not quite as consequential as in the ultimate performance situation.

Enhance Rehearsal with Feedback

Rehearsal works best when you can get feedback on your performance. For individuals trying to improve their global dexterity, two types of feedback are important. The first is the traditional type of feedback—what most people immediately think of. This is an evaluation of your *external performance* and how well you have performed the new cultural behaviors. That's certainly important because the ultimate purpose is to be effective in your cultural interactions. However, a second type of feedback is equally important for people learning to integrate these challenging new behaviors into their personal repertoires: *internal feedback* about how it feels, from a psychological perspective, to engage in the new cultural behaviors.

Does the level of expected directness that you have to exhibit in this situation to be effective in the new culture feel comfortable to you? If it does, that might mean that the adjustments you have made earlier to your behavior and to your perceptions of the behavior are working. If it doesn't, it might mean you need to tweak these adjustments and work on further customizing your behavior before proceeding through more rehearsal sequences. Let's see how Samuel used evaluation to help him develop cultural effectiveness.

It was 8:55 a.m.—just five minutes before the big brainstorming session. Samuel was certainly nervous, but also more confident than he had ever been about voicing his opinion in a roomful of senior colleagues. In the past, he would never have participated, figuring that his role was to listen and learn and to be polite and deferential while the more senior, experienced people made decisions. Now, he knew not only that it was perfectly appropriate and acceptable for him to speak up, but that his boss and the senior partners *expected* him to participate. In the past, the Nigerian voice in his head would have said: "Don't do it—be respectful. Speak when spoken to. Respect your elders." That voice was still there to some degree, but he had much more control over it. He was able to see that in a different country and culture it was OK for him to act differently, especially if the goal was to advance his professional career.

Samuel was successful in finding a way to be both appropriate and effective in the new culture and also feel inside as if he was not doing anything wrong—in fact, that he was actually doing something right: acting as a confident and capable professional and contributing in a significant way to the work of the firm.

The meeting turned out well—his first "performance" did not go perfectly, but it was good enough, and certainly better than his behavior in previous meetings. Samuel felt less self-conscious and more confident voicing his opinion and for the most part, felt that he did so in an effective manner.

Following the meeting, Samuel went back to his office to do a quick self-assessment of his performance. First, he made a quick assessment of his external performance—how he felt he did in the eyes of the other people in the room. Then he made an assessment of his internal performance—how it felt to engage in these new behaviors.

To assess his external performance, Samuel created a score-card for himself immediately after the meeting that captured how well he felt he did in accommodating to the American cultural code (figure 6-1). Then, later in the day, he was able to check these impressions with a senior partner at the meeting who was a mentor to him and who had agreed to help Samuel with his cultural adaptation.

FIGURE 6-1

Samuel's external scorecard

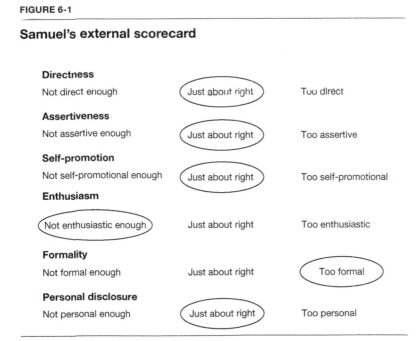

In thinking back to the meeting, Samuel thought that his level of directness and assertiveness was just about right. He had realized from his practice sessions the importance of injecting his voice and opinion into the discussion and how he often would not necessarily be "invited" to do so. As a result, he had practiced many different ways of getting his voice heard and of politely interrupting others in order to offer an opinion. He felt that he was not too intrusive in these interruptions, but also that he was not too reticent. So, on the assertiveness and directness scale, Samuel felt that he had done a commendable job. He also felt that his level of self-promotion was just about right. The session was not necessarily a context for explicit self-promotion, but the very act of more directly and assertively asserting his opinion was itself an act of self-promotion, so on that score as well, Samuel felt that his performance was satisfactory.

The trickiest parts of the situation were enthusiasm and formality, and in reflecting on his behavior, Samuel felt that next time he could be slightly more enthusiastic and slightly less formal in his communication. After all this time practicing and rehearsing and learning and justifying the new cultural code, Samuel still felt slightly awkward acting with the level of enthusiasm that his American colleagues exhibited. However, the good news was that he was acting with more enthusiasm than he had been previously. So, although perhaps not yet at the American level of appropriateness, Samuel's level of enthusiasm was approaching that mark.

Finally, he struggled in a similar way with formality. It was still difficult for Samuel to treat such senior members of the organization as colleagues, and he believed that he probably came off as slightly more formal than others might in this same situation. However, as was the case with enthusiasm, Samuel had improved his level of formality from previous trial runs and was acting in a far less formal manner than before, which he felt was very close to reaching the zone of appropriateness for American culture.

In addition to assessing his external performance, Samuel did a quick check of his internal state of mind, thinking about how it felt inside to adapt his behavior across each dimension of the cultural code (figure 6-2).

As is clear from his internal scorecard, Samuel's greatest struggle was with enthusiasm. In Nigeria, business meetings are far more formal and people behave in a far more subdued manner, especially when interacting with more senior members

FIGURE 6-2

Samuel's internal scorecard

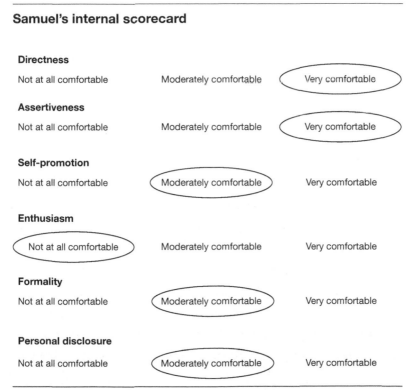

Directness

Not at all comfortable | Moderately comfortable | *Very comfortable*

Assertiveness

Not at all comfortable | Moderately comfortable | *Very comfortable*

Self-promotion

Not at all comfortable | *Moderately comfortable* | Very comfortable

Enthusiasm

Not at all comfortable | Moderately comfortable | Very comfortable

Formality

Not at all comfortable | *Moderately comfortable* | Very comfortable

Personal disclosure

Not at all comfortable | *Moderately comfortable* | Very comfortable of the organization. So, understandably, Samuel still found it difficult to interact with an American style of enthusiasm. But he was learning and improving, and overall felt quite pleased with how it went. So, overall, job well done!

YOUR TURN

Create Your Own Rehearsal Sequence

As you have seen in this chapter, it can be quite useful to integrate what you have learned through rehearsal and evaluation. Let's try it out for a situation of your own.

Name Your Situation

My situation is:

_____

_____

Act 1: Familiarization

This first stage entails "trying on" the new behaviors to see how they feel, outside of any formal practice or rehearsal context. People do this in a variety of ways. They practice by themselves, they write out a formal script, they look for examples on television, in the movies, or in real life to observe. They casually practice with friends or relatives or colleagues. They can shadow more experienced members of their organization. Can you think of ways that you might use the technique of familiarization to "try on" the new behaviors that you are learning to perform in your own professional life?

SAMPLE VERSION:

(using the situation of delivering negative feedback in Germany) I can observe how other German managers deliver feedback. I can try to imagine myself performing the same behavior and even write down a short script of what I might say.

YOUR VERSION:

_____

_____

Act 2: Rehearsal

Rehearsal is more formal than familiarization and entails taking what you have learned in this first stage and applying it to a more formalized practice session. You can do this with friends or colleagues playing the role of the other person (or people) in your situation. Can you think of ways that you might be able to create or take advantage of a rehearsal situation for yourself as you attempt to master your own foreign cultural behavior?

SAMPLE VERSION:

I can rehearse with other foreign-born colleagues who struggle with adapting their behavior in Germany. I might even find a German colleague who empathizes with my challenges and who can help me practice.

YOUR VERSION:

_____

_____

Act 3: Dress Rehearsal

This is the final practice run in a very realistic situation that is quite similar to the situation you are ultimately preparing for. People often try to find a "proxy" situation to do a dress rehearsal. This is a situation that is real and that has similar characteristics to the one you are ultimately preparing for. Can you think of ways that you might be able to conduct a dress rehearsal for practicing your own foreign cultural situation?

SAMPLE VERSION:

I can practice delivering negative feedback in brainstorming discussions with my closest German colleagues. It's a realistic situation, but because they are close colleagues and, in fact, understand the cultural difference I face in this situation, I feel more comfortable being frank with them than I do with my direct reports.

YOUR VERSION:

_____

_____

Personal Scorecard

When you actually try out your behavior in a real or realistic situation, use your personal scorecard to evaluate your performance on two different dimensions: externally in terms of the impression you likely created on others and internally in terms of how it felt to perform the behavior. For the external scorecard, you can also consult with a colleague or mentor to give you additional insight into how your performance was seen by others.

External Scorecard: Judge Your External Performance

For each dimension of the cultural code, circle how well you feel you performed, or, in the case of an external observer, how well that external observer felt you performed.

FIGURE 6-3

Your external scorecard

Directness

| Not direct enough | Just about right | Too direct |

Assertiveness

| Not assertive enough | Just about right | Too assertive |

Self-promotion

| Not self-promotional enough | Just about right | Too self-promotional |

Enthusiasm

| Not enthusiastic enough | Just about right | Too enthusiastic |

Formality

| Not formal enough | Just about right | Too formal |

Personal disclosure

| Not personal enough | Just about right | Too personal |

Internal Scorecard: Judge Your Internal Experience

For each dimension of the cultural code, circle how comfortable you felt inside when performing the behavior.

FIGURE 6-4

Your internal scorecard

Directness

Not at all comfortable   Moderately comfortable   Very comfortable

Assertiveness

Not at all comfortable   Moderately comfortable   Very comfortable

Self-promotion

Not at all comfortable   Moderately comfortable   Very comfortable

Enthusiasm

Not at all comfortable   Moderately comfortable   Very comfortable

Formality

Not at all comfortable   Moderately comfortable   Very comfortable

Personal disclosure

Not at all comfortable   Moderately comfortable   Very comfortable

PART THREE

Fine-Tuning Your Global Dexterity

You've mastered the basics. You understand how to diagnose the cultural code. You can see where your personal comfort zone meets the zone of appropriateness in the new culture and whether or not you need to switch your behavior to be appropriate and effective. You've learned about rehearsal and evaluation, about customizing your behavior, and about customizing and adjusting your perceptions.

You have clearly learned a great deal! However, as you undoubtedly have discovered, developing your global dexterity takes considerable effort and skill, and you can encounter challenges along the way. The purpose of this next section is to help you with these challenges. The advice is framed in terms of a set of dilemmas that people just like you have identified as key issues that they struggle with when learning to switch their cultural behavior.

1. How can I make sense of my progress in adapting my behavior over time?

2. How can I get others to forgive me for my cultural mistakes?

3. Is it worth having a mentor help me develop my global dexterity?

4. Do I adapt my behavior in every situation I encounter?

CHAPTER 7

Charting Your Progress
over Time

Think for a moment about all the personal interactions you experience during a given workweek. Chances are, the list is quite long: business meetings; brainstorming sessions; conversations with your boss, colleagues, and subordinates; touching base with suppliers, contacts, and customers; making small talk at lunch and dinner meetings and at networking events; asking for favors; providing help, giving and receiving feedback, and many more. In short, a myriad of situations.

Now, imagine yourself doing these very same activities but in a foreign cultural setting. Instead of meeting with your boss at home in the United States, Germany, or Canada, you are interacting with an Italian boss in Rome. Instead of meeting with American suppliers near your corporate headquarters, you are instead in Beijing meeting with potential Chinese suppliers. Instead of giving feedback to colleagues at home in Israel, you are giving feedback to colleagues in Seoul, Korea.

A common question people ask when developing new cultural skills is, quite simply, how to make sense of it all? How can we make sense of such varied experiences of adaptation across such a wide range of situations and contexts?

Your Personalized Portfolio of Cultural Adaptation

You may have a financial portfolio that consists of stocks and bonds, some of which thrive, and others of which struggle. Moreover, the performance of these stocks and bonds likely changes over time. What was once a low-performing stock might in a few months' time become a far more effective performer and so on.

Let's now take this analogy to the world of cultural adaptation: replace stocks and bonds with the range of different foreign cultural situations that you encounter in your work life. Each situation that you face in a foreign setting, ranging from performance feedback to participating in a business meeting, functions like an "asset" in your portfolio.

In your financial portfolio, you are always curious about the performance of your different assets. The same is true with the portfolio of situations that you face in a foreign culture. You can assess your experience of each foreign cultural situation in your overall portfolio by asking yourself two key diagnostic questions:

1. Do I feel authentic performing this behavior?
2. Can I perform the behavior successfully?

As we will see, the answer to these questions can often be quite different, even for the very same behavior.

Do I Feel Authentic Performing This Behavior?

Two main factors typically contribute to feelings of inauthenticity: how unfamiliar the behavior feels and whether it conflicts with your core values. Remember Tej, the Indian professional we met in chapter 3? In Tej's case, American-style networking behavior presented a strong challenge to her Indian cultural values of modesty and deference. This was because it required far more assertive, direct, and self-promotional behavior than she felt comfortable with, especially from having been born and raised in India and having internalized Indian cultural values.

Recall as well the case, in chapter 2, of Larry Campbell, the American manager in Germany who had to deliver negative feedback in a style that was far more direct and frank than he was used to and comfortable with. Larry also experienced a value conflict between how he had to act in Germany and his personal values concerning benevolence and kindness in his treatment of others. As a result of these value conflicts, Tej and Larry both felt disingenuous performing these new cultural behaviors.

You can also feel inauthentic because of how unfamiliar a new behavior feels, even if there is no value conflict. For example, if you are from a culture where a kiss on each cheek is not a typical greeting (e.g., many parts of the United States), it can feel inauthentic engaging in the behavior. It doesn't necessarily conflict with your values (unless, say, you come from a religious background that does not allow kissing between strangers or members of the opposite sex). It just feels inauthentic.

So, authenticity is the first dimension of your personal adaptation portfolio, and you can classify a particular behavior as being authentic or inauthentic for you.

Can I Perform the Behavior Successfully?

The second dimension to consider is *competence*: whether you can perform the behavior successfully, independent of authenticity. It may be the case, for example, that even though Tej feels disingenuous when performing networking behavior, she can actually do it quite effectively. Or perhaps Larry is actually quite skilled at delivering German-style feedback, even though he hates to do it because he feels inauthentic. We have all probably been in situations like that: where we are good at something, but don't necessarily feel ourselves when doing it. So, the second way to classify the situation is to ask yourself if you feel competent at behaving appropriately in it.

Assessing Your Authenticity and Competence in Specific Situations

When you assess a particular situation in terms of competence and authenticity at the same time, you can use the matrix in figure 7-1 to classify the situation as belonging to one of four quadrants.[1]

In the upper left-hand quadrant is the *comfort zone*. This is reserved for situations where you feel authentic and competent at the same time. These are the easiest and most natural

FIGURE 7-1

Adaptation matrix

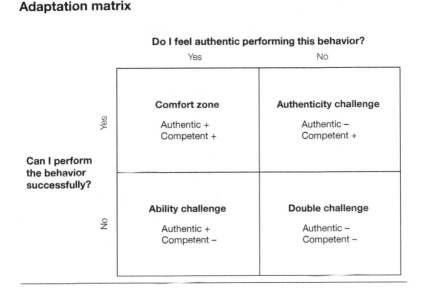

behaviors for you in a foreign culture, the ones that either require little work or that have become comfortable after you have done a great deal of work making yourself feel authentic and act competently. The upper right-hand corner of the grid is the *authenticity challenge* zone: you feel competent performing a particular behavior, but not authentic. These are situations where you don't lack skill—you know how you are supposed to perform—but you feel disingenuous performing them. In the lower left-hand corner is the *ability challenge* zone. Here, you feel relatively authentic performing the behavior, but lack the skill to perform it with a high level of competence. The bottom right-hand corner—the *double challenge* zone—is the most difficult place to be. In double challenge situations, you feel incompetent and inauthentic at the same time.

Create Your Own Personal Portfolio of Cultural Adaptation

You can use this framework to assess any situation or set of situations that you currently face in cross-cultural work. So let's give it a try. Take a pen and, in the "List of Key Challenges" below or on a separate piece of paper, write down five to ten key situations that you currently face while doing business in a particular foreign culture, or that you have faced or will face. I've provided an example of ten situations that an American-born manager might struggle with in her work in Brazil. You can use this illustration to inspire your own list. After completing the list, you'll have a chance to place each situation in your personal cultural adaptation portfolio.

List of Key Challenges

Sample challenges: An American-born manager in Brazil

1. Making small talk with colleagues

2. Giving feedback to my boss

3. Giving a formal presentation at a meeting

4. Receiving a compliment from a colleague

5. Pitching my idea to investors

6. Interviewing for a job

7. Promoting myself at networking events

8. Asking a favor from a colleague

9. Getting my voice heard during a meeting

10. Telling a joke at lunch

YOUR VERSION:

1. _____

2. _____

3. _____

4. _____

5. _____

Once you've created your list, place each one of the situations (or use the item number from the list) in one of the four quadrants in your personal cultural adaptation portfolio (figure 7-2).

FIGURE 7-2

My personal cultural adaptation portfolio

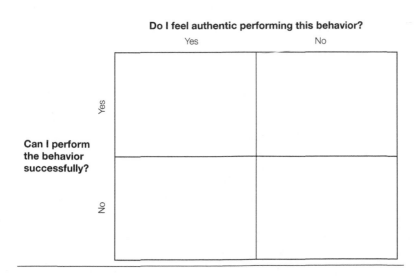

The first thing you will likely notice from this exercise is that your experiences abroad are typically not homogeneous (unless you have purposefully chosen only the easiest or most difficult situations to focus on), and that you're quite likely to have situations in more than one quadrant—maybe even in all four quadrants. This itself is often a major insight for people who often characterize their experiences abroad in monolithic terms: as being uniformly "easy" or "difficult." And now that you've created your portfolio, you can consider which need to be addressed and how you might do so. For example, in situations where you struggle with competence, but not authenticity, you can focus attention on building knowledge and skill. Or, when the main challenge is authenticity rather than competence, you can use customization techniques to reduce the level of identity and value conflict you experience, as discussed in chapter 5.

Finally, you can also use your personalized cultural adaptation portfolio to track your experience of cultural adaptation over time. As a thought exercise, imagine where the five to ten situations that you listed would have been when you first started working in the foreign culture you're thinking about. Compare that to now. Have any of the situations changed quadrants?

Consider, for example, Samuel, the Nigerian consultant we met in chapter 6 who was learning to participate in brainstorming meetings with his senior American colleagues. At the beginning, Samuel was in the double challenge zone for brainstorming, as indicated in figure 7-3. He felt incompetent performing the behaviors necessary for participating

FIGURE 7-3

Samuel's original adaptation portfolio

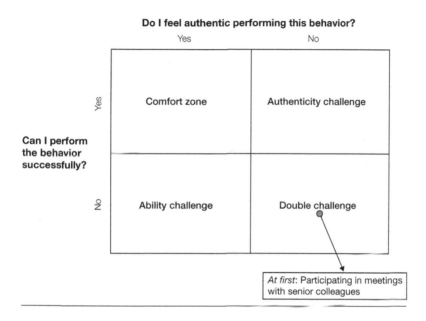

Do I feel authentic performing this behavior?

	Yes	No
Can I perform the behavior successfully? Yes	Comfort zone	Authenticity challenge
No	Ability challenge	Double challenge

At first: Participating in meetings with senior colleagues

effectively in these situations and also felt inauthentic because these behaviors were in conflict with his culturally ingrained values and beliefs.

However, over time and through the hard work of learning the cultural rules and practicing the behavior in a variety of ways, Samuel was able to improve his level of comfort and competence. Over time he transitioned far closer to being in the middle of the comfort zone, where he felt both competent and authentic engaging in the behavior (see figure 7-4).

FIGURE 7-4

Samuel's adaptation portfolio after practice

The same can be true for you. With hard work and discipline, you can transform your experience of cultural adaptation in a very short time. What this portfolio framework does is provide you with a tool to help you chart your progress over time throughout this journey.

CHAPTER 8

Getting Others to Forgive Your Cultural Mistakes

Imagine the following situation: Mark de Jong, a Dutch-born consultant in New York, makes finishing touches to his PowerPoint presentation and starts to smile: this is going to be his American "coming-out party." Following university in Amsterdam, Mark had been working for three years in the Netherlands for a European-based management consulting firm. Mark had delivered plenty of presentations to colleagues and clients in the Netherlands and in Europe. Now he found himself for the first time in New York, about to deliver his first American-style presentation. But, from his experience watching Americans present on videoconferences and in person, he had a pretty good idea of the cultural differences.

From what he had seen, Americans seemed to be much more informal than the Dutch—and certainly the Germans with whom Mark also did a lot of business. It seemed common to tell a joke or two at the beginning of the presentation, and perhaps even have a *Dilbert* cartoon as one of the opening slides. Mark also noticed that the American consultants were much more emotionally expressive, enthusiastic, and animated during their presentations. They would exaggerate far more than the Dutch, who were more even-keeled when presenting. At first, he found the American approach superficial and very—well—*American*. But after a while, he started to appreciate the approach and even looked forward to the joking and informality.

The big day had come, and it was now his turn to turn on the charm and deliver the presentation. To get himself in character, he had an extra shot of espresso and smiled at himself in the mirror. He knew he could do this. Although it felt weird at first to be so animated and casual—almost like a stand-up comic—he had convinced himself that it was expected.

Needless to say, Mark was shocked to learn how poorly his presentation was received when he huddled with his colleagues after the meeting. It seemed that Mark went a bit overboard. If, on a ten-point scale, the Dutch style for this presentation was a 2 on enthusiasm and informality, the American style for this type of professional presentation would be around a 4 or a 5. Mark had inadvertently overshot the mark and produced a 7. He felt very embarrassed and wondered whether he would ever be able to recover from this cultural faux pas.

Unfortunately, cultural mistakes are inevitable. In an ideal world, we would wait to unveil our new cultural skills until we were 100 percent ready. We would practice for days, weeks—years, if necessary—until everything was perfect. Then, and only then, would we go out into the world and use our new skills. The reality, of course, is that this is rarely the case. We often have to perform in important professional situations abroad without a perfect mastery of the new cultural code, and we will undoubtedly make errors. And these errors can prove to be quite costly.

Take the case of Eric Rivers, the American executive profiled in chapter 1. His failure to adapt his behavior caused him to lose the trust and respect of his Indian subordinates. In other cases presented in this book, the failure to act with global dexterity has threatened people's ability to impress colleagues and contacts or win the support, respect, and trust of subordinates and superiors.

How Can We Be Forgiven for Our Cultural Mistakes?

The ability to adapt successfully is critical for doing business in a foreign setting, and poor adaptation can be a serious liability. Yet, the practical problem for professionals doing business abroad is that these mistakes are inevitable. The question is whether there is a way to get people to forgive us for the cultural mistakes that we inevitably make.

Location, Location, Location . . .

Interestingly, a major factor impacting forgiveness is entirely outside of our control. It has to do with *where*—in which country—the cultural mistake takes place. According to fascinating cross-cultural research by Michele Gelfand from the University of Maryland and her colleagues, it turns out that certain countries are more forgiving of cultural breaches than others. If you commit a faux pas in a "tight" society, such as Pakistan, Malaysia, or Singapore, for example, chances are that you will not be forgiven for your mistake—at least not as readily as you would be in a "looser," more forgiving society such as Iceland, France, Hong Kong, Belgium, or the United States.[1]

The tightness or looseness of a society is deeply rooted in that society's historical background and political structure. Tight societies are more likely to have autocratic political systems, restricted media, and strong criminal justice systems with harsh punishments. Looser societies have more open, democratic governments; comparatively less severe political systems, open media, and people have more power to dissent.[2]

Adjusting Your "Foreignness"

Something you have slightly more control over is how "foreign" you are perceived to be by others in the local setting. Sometimes when others perceive you as foreign, they will forgive your cultural mistakes that you commit. The logic is similar to that of a novice driver with a "student driver" sign on top of the car, or someone manning the checkout counter wearing a "cashier in training" badge. When you are perceived to be foreign, you are given a bit of leeway when you make mistakes.

Consider the case of Haruhiko, a Japanese manager who was struggling to learn how to communicate appropriately with his superiors in Japanese. In Japan, there is a set of very specific and subtle verbal and nonverbal signals that you must master in order to communicate with people up and down the organizational hierarchy. Master these signals and you can seamlessly operate in a Japanese organization. But if you fail to do so, you will be seen as a bull in a china shop: clumsy and culturally inappropriate.

Haruhiko's problem was that, although he was Japanese and spoke Japanese without an accent, he had actually grown up in Italy, so he did not know these corporate-specific communication signals. But because this wasn't apparent from his looks or speech, people were shocked and disappointed by his cultural incompetence. It proved to be a major liability. So Haruhiko had to concoct a plan for forgiveness. In the end, he came up with something simple, but very effective. He decided to accentuate his foreignness: to make it clear to his Japanese colleagues that, despite appearances, he actually was not from the culture originally and therefore deserved patience and forgiveness for his cultural errors.

The first thing he did was to change his name. Instead of using his Japanese name, Haruhiko, he started using his Italian name, Claudio. It was odd at first, because he wanted so badly to accommodate to the Japanese culture, but it actually worked. It served as a cue for people to pause and reflect on the fact that he might not be from Japan and that there might be an explanation for the cultural faux pas that he was committing. Haruhiko also started wearing Western suits and more colorful ties than the Japanese were accustomed to—again to accentuate his foreignness. In the end, these very subtle changes worked magic. Haruhiko was granted forgiveness and was able to continue working on the subtleties of Japanese corporate culture without being punished for mistakes committed in the learning process.

THE POTENTIAL DOWNSIDES OF SIGNALING FOREIGNNESS

Although it was helpful in Haruhiko's case, signaling foreignness can be tricky business because our foreignness means so many different things to different people. In some cases, foreignness clearly helps us, as Haruhiko's situation illustrated. When we signal to others that we are not from a given culture, we provide a built-in excuse for why we might not act in an acceptable manner, and to the extent that a person "buys" this excuse, we can be forgiven for the cultural faux pas that we commit.

However, at the same time, being seen as foreign can also potentially hurt us. Take, for example, the case of language fluency, which is perhaps the most common way that we communicate our foreignness in another culture. By speaking the foreign language with an accent or with a low level of fluency, we indicate to others—in most cases inadvertently—that we are not from the culture. Does this poor fluency help us when it comes to others' evaluations of our cultural missteps?

A few years ago I conducted a research study to test this very question.[3] The context was Russians learning to interview for jobs in the United States. For the study, Russian job candidate Sergei acted either appropriately or inappropriately in the job interview and spoke with either a high degree of fluency in English or a low degree of fluency in English. The question was whether Sergei's lack of fluency would serve as a "cue" to his foreignness and therefore cut him slack for the cultural faux pas that he committed—or whether there might be a hidden downside to speaking with a low level of language fluency.

To test this question, I created a series of videotaped versions of Sergei acting appropriately or inappropriately during an American employment interview and varied how fluently he spoke the language. In some cases he spoke quite fluently and in other cases much less so.

Interviewer: So, Sergei, any trouble with our directions to the office today?

Sergei: Yes.

Interviewer: I see here that you come from Russia?

Sergei: Yes.

Interviewer: Ah, so how do you like living in Boston so far?

Sergei: I don't like.

Interviewer: OK. And how about weaknesses? What would you say are your weaknesses as a worker?

Sergei: Sometimes I do not like to work with other people.

Interviewer: OK. Well, do you have any questions for me?

Sergei: How much per hour?

So, was the low-fluency or high-fluency Sergei more positively perceived during this awkward interview? The answer was the low-fluency Sergei—but only in terms of how likeable he was perceived to be. When Sergei made these mistakes, he was seen as more likeable when he did so with poor fluency. People felt sorry for him and understood that he was from another culture and apparently did not know any better. However, at the same time that they saw him as more likeable, they also saw him as less competent. It was a double-edged sword.

You can imagine other features of language operating in a similar way. For example, if you speak a foreign language with a strong accent, that may explain your cultural mistake to people and you may, in a sense, be forgiven. However, at the same time, you may also fall prey to stereotypes about your accent that you have no control over.

What's the moral of the story? Signaling foreignness matters—sometimes a great deal. But, the effects are not uniformly positive, and unfortunately, you don't always have total control over these effects.

Increasing the Odds of Being Forgiven for Your Cultural Mistakes

If foreignness and location both matter, but you don't have much control over them, what *is* under your control to increase the odds of being forgiven by others for cultural miscues that you commit? There are three potential things that you can do to cut yourself slack for your cultural mistakes. These strategies are:

- Showing genuine interest in the other culture
- Deflecting attention away from yourself by "blaming" your native culture
- Building a relationship

Strategy #1: Show Genuine Interest in the
Other Culture

The first thing under your control is, quite simply, your ability
to show genuine interest in the other person's culture. Show
that you care, that you are sincerely trying to learn the other
person's culture. Chances are, if people sense your authenticity,
you will be forgiven for your mistakes. Kostas, the Greek
professional working in Luxembourg, whose story you might
remember from chapter 5, likened showing interest in a new
culture to making deposits in a forgiveness bank account.
If you demonstrate to people in the other culture that you
respect their culture, they will develop a positive attitude
toward you. This goodwill will grow over time and buffer you
from costly faux pas. Instead of being punished, you will be
seen as having made an honest mistake because you are clearly
interested in the culture and trying to accommodate your
behavior.

There are dozens of ways to express such sincere interest.
For Kostas, it was learning the Luxembourgish language.
Although it is quite difficult and unique—a variant of high
German spoken by only 300,000 people in the world—it was
not particularly difficult for Kostas, who spoke five other lan-
guages fluently. For others who are not such skilled linguists,
there are different paths and possibilities for demonstrating
interest. A senior executive at a *Fortune* 500 company, for
example, used his love of sports as a vehicle for showing interest in other cultures. At a leadership development retreat in
India, he was able to forge bonds with his Indian colleagues by
getting them to teach him about cricket. He had never played

or watched cricket before—and probably never would have if he had never traveled to India. But he was genuinely interested in sports, and in making a personal connection to the culture, and his Indian colleagues could clearly sense this. The key is to find something that works for you—some aspect of the new culture that you can plug into; something that interests you and about which you can express your interest to others. If it's genuine, people will notice.

Strategy #2: Deflect Attention from Yourself by "Blaming" Your Native Culture

This can be a tricky strategy, but if it's within your repertoire, this strategy can actually work wonders. Forgive yourself by blaming your culture. In other words, it's not your fault you acted in a certain culturally inappropriate way—it's the fault of the culture you come from!

Let me explain with an example. I was recently speaking with a cultural communication specialist who frequently witnesses this strategy in action among her Brazilian clients who are interviewing for jobs in the United States. Many have a tendency to speak a great deal in interviews: to go on and on—well beyond the point of appropriateness for the interview situation. Many of these clients actually know this about themselves, but have a hard time self-regulating.

So, what do they do? To excuse themselves, some clients will point out the faux pas, apologize, and, then, with a twinkle in their eye, blame their Brazilian background for "taking over." They might say something like: "I'm sorry, I know I'm speaking too much. My Brazilian side is coming out again!" Or,

"I know I'm speaking a lot. It's my Brazilian nature. Let me give you a chance to talk!"

The key, of course, is that you need to be aware of your miscue in the first place to pull off this strategy, and you also need to be able to refer to the gaffe in a humorous and self-deprecating manner. It can be tricky, especially if the mistake is something that truly upsets the other person. In that case, it might be an unwise strategy. But for a minor mistake, the strategy can work well, and in the case of the Brazilian clients, it worked wonders.

Another example of this same strategy comes from Marco, whom we met in chapter 2—the Italian COO working in India. Marco frequently finds himself blaming his "Italian heritage" for mistakes, especially when he makes off-color or risqué jokes, which can be taboo in the Indian cultural context. But he acknowledges such gaffes, explicitly blaming his Italian heritage for "taking control." And believe it or not, the strategy works. His "Italian side" is "punished," but he's left untarnished—given license to engage in the otherwise inappropriate behavior because he essentially had no choice—as if he were being controlled by a higher power.

As you can see, blaming your cultural background can work, but only if the audience is receptive and, perhaps most importantly, if you have the charisma and charm to pull it off. Otherwise it can really backfire. Think about a stereotypical "ugly American" butchering the cultural rules of another society and then, loudly and without any charm or charisma, saying something like: "Forgive me, it's my American heritage that is causing me to act in this way!" You can imagine how this might be received.

Strategy #3: Build a Relationship

Blaming your cultural heritage is tricky and depends on your ability to charm your counterpart. However, not all of us are so charming, and it's easy to picture many contexts where offended colleagues will not stand for culturally unacceptable behavior, even if you try to excuse it. What should you do in these situations? Try changing the nature of the relationship! Strong interpersonal relationships are perhaps the single most powerful tool for softening the blow of a cultural faux pas. As a suspicious outsider, you may be punished for making a mistake; however, as a cherished colleague or friend, you will likely be supported, rather than punished, for your efforts—albeit imperfect—at cultural accommodation.

Marcel, a German executive working for a *Fortune* 500 company based in the United States, is quite blunt and direct in his communication style. What has been quite helpful for Marcel, however, has been the relationships he's built with American-born colleagues who have become aware of his style and of his efforts—albeit often unsuccessful—to adapt to US conventions. When he commits a faux pas, his colleagues see the mistake in the context of Marcel's efforts to learn the culture. They judge the faux pas much less harshly than they would if Marcel were outside of such a collaborative, supportive context.

One day, as Marcel was walking to a meeting down the central corridor of corporate headquarters, he saw his close American colleague, John, along with his wife, who was visiting for the day. As soon as John saw Marcel in the hallway, he exclaimed "Marcel!" in an extremely friendly tone, slowing down and starting to introduce his wife. "Marcel, I'd like you to meet my wife, Nancy! We're going down for lunch right now. Are you interested in joining us?" Most Americans in this situation would stop and chat and perhaps gracefully decline the invitation. Marcel took a different tack. He stopped for a split second, looked at John, and said, quite abruptly, "No, I want to go to the gym" before continuing down the hall.

Anyone else in this situation—me included—would have been pretty annoyed. But John just laughed, joking back to Marcel: "Now, that was pretty clear!" And that's when Marcel realized his faux pas. He quickly recovered, walked back to greet John and his wife, and suggested getting together for coffee instead. The relationship between John and Marcel saved the day. It created a context within which Marcel could be forgiven for the cultural mistake. If this were anyone else, Marcel would have likely not been able to recover so quickly and the faux pas could have led to a damaged relationship. With John, however, it was not a problem.

So, the bottom line is that you *can* find ways to be forgiven for the cultural faux pas that you inevitably commit. I have detailed many such strategies, but you may also develop some strategies of your own. They may not work forever: at some point, people's expectations may change, and they may feel that you have been in a culture long enough that you are expected to adapt effectively, no matter what. But I have found that people generally will cut you slack, especially if you show interest in their culture, signal your foreignness, and work on developing a strong interpersonal connection.

CHAPTER 9

Finding a Cultural Mentor

Hideaki Kazama took a close look at the impressive display of holiday treats at the company party and decided he wasn't hungry. It was 3 p.m. in the United States, but 5 a.m. in Japan, and despite the fact that he had already been in the United States for two weeks, Hideaki's body had still not yet fully acclimated to American time. Hideaki was taking part in a special leadership training program organized by his company for people they had designated as high-potential employees. After the two-year stint in the United States, Hideaki would go back to Japan and be on the fast track to upper management. In fact, many of the top people in the company had been on this leadership track and that's why Hideaki was so excited to follow in his colleagues' footsteps.

Hideaki was very confident about his technical skills, but less certain of his cultural skills. That's why he selected an American colleague, Tom, who could be a role model for him—someone whose behavior he could emulate to get off on the right foot with his new American colleagues. Tom, whose cubicle was next to Hideaki's, seemed to be pretty effective in the US setting. Hideaki noticed, for example, how Tom had no trouble interrupting others at business meetings, something that Hideaki found extremely difficult to do. Tom was also very vocal in social situations, speaking loudly and confidently, and Hideaki was impressed how he really was able to command people's attention.

So Hideaki took a leap and patterned his behavior after his new American colleague, even though Tom's style was so different from Hideaki's natural style. For example, in one case, Hideaki vehemently argued with his colleagues and new bosses about continuing to test a particular programming code, even after all others in the room, including his boss and his boss's boss, advocated for a "code freeze"—meaning that no additional features would be added.

In Japan, he probably would never had said anything in the first place, but he knew he needed to be strong and assertive to succeed in the United States. So Hideaki did not back down, vehemently arguing the case way past the point of appropriateness. It was truly a cringeworthy moment, but Hideaki unfortunately did not realize this until well after the damage had been done. As soon as he recognized that he had made a cardinal error in judgment and had acted in a wildly inappropriate manner, Hideaki slouched down in his chair, utterly embarrassed. He never did recover from this mistake, and in fact, ended up going back to Japan early.

Hideaki's story highlights the importance of finding someone in a foreign culture who can help develop your global dexterity. If you choose wisely, such a person can be an extremely valuable resource. If you end up choosing poorly, however, this person can end up doing more damage than good.

Choosing a Model: The Importance of Picking the Right Person

Technically speaking, Tom was a model rather than a mentor for Hideaki. There is a big difference between the two and it's important to understand as you consider how other people might help you improve your global dexterity. A *model* is someone whose behavior you emulate. Modeling entails watching how someone else does something and patterning your behavior accordingly. When you model your behavior after someone, you use that person as a guide.

Modeling is something you have done all your life. It is one of the main ways that we learn the rules for appropriate behavior within our own native cultural settings. We watch other people behave in the world—especially our parents and older siblings—and we observe the effectiveness of their actions. We see what seems to work, what doesn't, and over time develop our own personal styles. In the cross-cultural realm, someone like Hideaki can observe someone like Tom performing behavior in different situations, draw conclusions about the effectiveness of that behavior and then pattern his own behavior after the model.

As you can see from Hideaki's situation, however, modeling can be fraught with difficulties, especially if you choose the wrong person to emulate. Hideaki clearly chose poorly, since Tom's behavior was actually quite inappropriate within the

American cultural setting. So take note: the first, very important question for people looking to emulate others in foreign cultural settings is: How can you choose the right person to emulate if you don't know the culture to begin with?

There's no perfect formula, but here are two specific things you can do to increase the chances of finding an appropriate model. The first is to observe multiple people. Hideaki was so anxious to act American right away that he neglected to consider the range of behavior in the new setting before crafting his own approach. If Hideaki had looked at the behaviors of multiple potential models and compared them with each other, he might have learned that Tom's behavior—although consistent with Hideaki's naive stereotypes of effective American behavior—was actually quite ineffective within the US culture. He would have learned that Tom indeed commanded attention, but in a bad way; that what appeared to be confidence was hubris; and that what seemed to be assertiveness was aggressiveness.

The second tip is to use the time that you have to your advantage. In some cases, you might not have the time to observe and compare the styles of multiple people, but if you do, use it to compare, contrast, and then to build your own style from a compilation of what you observe. In fact, that's just what Yuji, Hideaki's colleague, did in a situation very similar to Hideaki's. Yuji was also in the United States as part of the same leadership development cohort, but took a very different approach toward crafting his new cultural style. Instead of immediately selecting a model, Yuji waited, carefully observing several different people over a two- to three-week period, and only then sculpted an approach of his own from what he had observed. Yuji's approach was just the sort of blend that I have been describing throughout this book: something that fit within his own personal comfort zone, but which also was appropriate in the United States, and which also reflected elements of the styles of many of the different people he observed. The moral of the story: take the time to observe multiple people when crafting your own personal approach. It's well worth the effort.

Working with a Mentor

Both Yuji and Hideaki used modeling as their tool for adjusting behavior. A very different approach is to find a *cultural mentor*: someone you work with one-on-one to improve your cultural skills, and who can provide this type of guidance on an ongoing basis. This was just what Rick Perlin needed when he went to Asia for the first time as the head of marketing for a *Fortune* 500 consumer goods company. Rick was a top-notch marketer and an excellent manager, but had never been abroad for more than a week. Luckily, Rick was aware of this deficiency and of the need for help, so as soon as he landed in Hong Kong, one of the first things he did was look for an informal cultural mentor: someone who could school him in the subtleties of communicating in the new culture—how to interact with peers and subordinates, how to communicate with his boss, how to greet and interact with colleagues, even how to seat people at a business meeting. Luckily, Rick was able to quickly establish a relationship with one of his new colleagues, who ended up serving as a mentor to him. For example, it turned out that there is a very specific protocol for where people sit at meetings in the Hong Kong office: the two most senior people from each company usually are seated next to each other, across the from the door, and the people from each company are seated to the sides of their respective bosses at increasingly lower levels of hierarchy. This is something Rick never would have known, and he was tremendously grateful to have a mentor to help him with such culturally specific details.

The Role of Good Mentors: Provide Information and Offer Support

Mentors typically serve two different functions for the people they work with: an informational function, providing helpful advice and feedback to improve cross-cultural skills, and a psychological function, providing supportive and encouraging feedback and guidance about the emotional side of cultural adaptation, helping their protégés grapple with the different psychological challenges that they face when adapting cultural behavior. Mentors can come from inside the firm—as was the case with Rick Perlin, or they can also come from outside the firm—and each model has its strengths and liabilities.

Insider mentors, like the one Rick worked with, are typically "low cost," in the sense that you do not need to hire them or pay for their services. They also can have relevant knowledge about the very particular context you are operating in—and therefore may implicitly understand certain challenges that you face in that setting, and can counsel you about these challenges more easily than an outsider could.

One liability of an insider mentor, however, is confidentiality, especially if you feel uncomfortable revealing the true extent of your cultural deficiencies with an insider mentor. For example, what if you struggle with certain types of behavior that you do not necessarily want revealed to an insider mentor, no matter how much you trust or respect that person?

For that reason, people often also go outside the organization to find a cultural mentor. For example, I was recently speaking with a Swedish CEO who does extensive business in Japan. The CEO was quite cosmopolitan and easily interacts across various different European countries, but at the same time, he did not necessarily want to reveal what might be perceived as a weakness. Thus, he ended up hiring an outside consultant to serve as his mentor—a former CEO turned consultant who had lived and worked in Japan for many years, and who could identify with the challenges of being a foreigner negotiating with the Japanese while also offering wise counsel about the best ways to approach the challenge.

I also recently had the opportunity to perform the function of an outside mentor myself for a Chinese-born consultant in the United States who was struggling to learn how to adapt his behavior when making small talk in American business situations. The consultant, whom I will call Tong, was quite experienced, with twelve years of consulting experience under his belt, and many successful years at his US-based firm. The problem was that Tong wanted to make partner, and to achieve this level, he needed to be more than just an excellent technician. He had to become a rainmaker who could woo clients and bring in business. And this is where small talk came in.

Tong noticed how the most successful partners at the firm weren't necessarily as technically savvy as he was. However, they were interpersonally savvy, able to easily converse with others and forge close relationships. Tong desperately wanted to do this as well.

Think about any relationship you have—with your boss, your colleagues, or your spouse. All of these relationships begin with small talk. Although the actual topics discussed might be unimportant, the connection that is built is tremendously important. If you can make small talk in a culturally appropriate style, you have a leg up as a foreigner in the United States. You can build relationships with your boss, colleagues, and clients that are critical for advancing in your career.

But Tong struggled when making small talk. One difficulty was sharing personal information with strangers. In China, talk between strangers is far less personally revealing than in the United States. But in America, Tong had to learn to be comfortable sharing his personal opinions and perspectives. Tong knew that revealing something about himself was a critical part of creating a personal bond, but he didn't feel comfortable doing it. The other aspect of small talk that Tong struggled with was actually ending the small-talk in conversations. Tong had a very difficult time trying to end a conversation and move on to talk to another person, which was a critical skill at networking events or at industry get-togethers. Whenever he tried to end a conversation, Tong felt guilty: as if he were being impolite and also disappointing the other person he was speaking with.

As a mentor, I worked with Tong on both of these issues. For personal disclosure, we worked on customizing the sorts of things that Tong would feel comfortable discussing and what for him personally would be taboo. Similarly, we worked on scripting different ways he might end conversations, trying them out in practice sessions with just me and also with some of his work colleagues, and then adjusting to make an even closer fit with his personal preferences. In addition to customizing behavior, we also worked on customizing perceptions. I explained to Tong why, from the perspective of his likely US counterpart, it was appropriate and even expected to contribute personal stories and anecdotes and to express personal opinions and preferences. It made the other person feel he was getting to know and like Tong and resulted in a far more personal and memorable connection.

In addition to providing Tong with this information, I was also able to serve as an emotional support. Although I am not Chinese and cannot fully empathize with the challenges that someone like Tong faces, I was familiar with the challenges of adapting behavior in general, and could help Tong notice the challenges he was facing and develop ways of coping with them. Tong had internal mentors in his company who could help him with other aspects of the cultural adaptation process, but these particular psychological challenges were well suited to an outside person like myself who could provide expert, confidential advice and counsel to Tong as he worked on developing his cultural skills.

Find a Mentor or Model Who Can Appreciate the Challenges You Face

Tong's story is illustrative of two key roles a mentor can play: a rich source of information about the new culture, the rules for appropriate behavior, and how others in the new culture expect you to behave, which can be quite important for helping people rationalize behavior that on the face of it feels inappropriate or illegitimate. The second is as a source of support and comfort: someone who can empathize with the challenges of adapting cultural behavior and help someone grapple with these challenges.

Who can play such a mentoring role? Just about anyone familiar with the new culture. It could be someone who is native to the new culture, as I was for Tong, or Dave was for Rick. Or, as in the Swedish CEO's case, a mentor could be someone who has lived in the new culture longer than you have and who has endured and overcome challenges similar to those you face. In fact, such a person can be the ideal type of mentor: someone just like you who can speak from a position of real authority and legitimacy as a fellow, but more experienced non-native.

The single most important characteristic, however, whether the person is native- or non-native-born is *empathy*. The best mentor is someone who gets the challenges and can help you learn to manage them. A knowledgeable, empathic cultural mentor can be a tremendously helpful resource during the cultural adaptation process.

CHAPTER 10

Choosing Whether or Not to Adapt Your Behavior

You've learned a lot about diagnosing, adapting, and customizing cultural behaviors. But it's important to remember that switching cultural behavior is a *choice*, and a choice that only you can make. As we have seen throughout the book, people decide to switch their behaviors all the time because it helps them develop professionally and achieve many important personal and professional goals. However, in certain situations—for ethical or moral reasons, or because behaviors may conflict with your professional goals—you may have to make the choice not to adapt to new cultural norms.

When Cultural Norms Conflict with Morals and Ethics

Sometimes the course of action you're expected to take is not only inauthentic, but actually comes into conflict with your moral code. How will you choose to respond in such situations? Consider the following examples drawn from managers and executives' real-life experiences.

Charles's Story: Preserving Human Dignity

One afternoon at work, Charles, an American-born executive at a Mumbai-based software company, was meeting with his new Indian colleagues in the executive boardroom. At the beginning of the meeting, a young man, who couldn't have been more than sixteen years old, walked into the room to serve them tea, and when it was his turn, Charles accepted the tea, and offered a quiet "Thank you" to the boy.

What happened next was shocking—at least to Charles. As soon as the boy left, the executives in the room stared at Charles as if he had committed the most egregious faux pas one could imagine. What did he do? What could have gone wrong?

As it turns out, Charles's cultural mistake was something he never could have anticipated: it was thanking the tea boy, who came from the "untouchable" caste of Indian society. In India, as Charles learned, people from this caste were to be ignored completely—as if they did not exist. By acknowledging the boy's existence, Charles had committed a faux pas.[1]

As he considered the situation and realized that he would have many more meetings in India with colleagues and with tea boys, Charles realized that he had a choice to make. Was he going to adapt his behavior in this situation and act as the Indian executives did? Or was he going to be his authentic self in this situation, thanking the tea boy and perhaps in the process offending his Indian colleagues?

Although thanking the tea boy was not core to his business, it was core to Charles in a different way because adapting his behavior in this situation would mean compromising his moral and ethical standards. Violating his culturally ingrained values and beliefs was one thing, and he was willing to do this in order to accommodate behavior to the Indian workplace. However, morals and ethics were different, and that's where he drew the line. He therefore made the conscious choice *not* to adapt his behavior. In the end, he was willing to endure any collateral damage from breaching this Indian convention because it was so abhorrent to him. Secretly, he also hoped that his actions might one day inspire his Indian colleagues to do the same.

Nancy's Story: A Question of Personal Dignity

Another example of a person making a similar ethically driven choice not to adapt is Nancy Chen, a thirty-two-year-old marketing manager from the United States at a major industrial products company. A few years ago, Nancy was in Singapore with two of her colleagues for an important negotiation with a key supplier. After a long day at the negotiating table, Nancy and her team sat down with their Singaporean counterparts for dinner and drinks. As Nancy tells the story: "We were just sitting there, starting the dinner and making pleasantries, when a jovial and rather loud Chinese Singaporean gentleman from the other side gets everyone's attention, looks in my direction, and says 'You're attractive. I'd like to take you to this club I belong to. I want to show you around and have them see you.'" Needless to say, Nancy was shocked—as were her American colleagues, who were so embarrassed for Nancy that they would not even look in her direction. How should she respond? How could anyone respond to a comment like that?

One possible response would be to "act Asian," which in this situation meant saying nothing and averting her eyes. It certainly would not be Nancy's instinctive response, which was to tell the man off or perhaps to get up and leave the room. As a proud Asian American businesswoman who had struggled with more subtle forms of sexism in rising to her present position, she was simply unwilling to accommodate. It violated her internal moral code of behavior. But acting out and unleashing her anger was also probably not the ideal response, as it would undoubtedly ruin all the hard work her team had accomplished in Singapore. In Asian business culture, it was very uncommon for women to act assertively with men or to contradict them in public.

Nancy ended up not switching to an Asian style. Instead, she used humor to defuse the situation. Seething inside but unwilling to let her anger show in any way, Nancy smiled broadly, looked the man straight in the eye, and said: "Yes! I think that's a great idea! In fact it's *such* a great idea that I think we should go right now." She got up, took his hand, and started to walk out the door. It was a shocking gesture that caught the attention of everyone in the room. At that point, the man let go of her hand and looked at her. Then he let out the deepest, loudest laugh Nancy had ever heard, sat down, and continued his meal. The very next morning, Nancy and her team concluded the deal and were on a plane back to the United States.

Amy's Story: Confronting Questionable
Business Practices

Nancy and Charles decided not to use their powers of global dexterity because adapting behavior in their minds in these specific situations would have conflicted with their own moral codes. In other cases, the conflict is not only with their own moral code, but also with the moral code of the company. Take, for example, the case of Amy King, a Canadian-born executive at a major global consumer products company in the United States whose company sells products around the world. A key goal of any consumer products company is to secure prime space on the shelves of the most desirable retail locations, and that goal was front and center in Amy's mind when she started her job as the product manager for one of her company's best-selling worldwide brands.

One day on the very first week in her job, Amy received a call from Maxim Shirokov, a newly hired local manager in Moscow. The purpose of the call was to "meet" Amy virtually, and to also inquire about how she wanted to handle the "motivation money" for the Moscow market—which meant the bribes necessary for securing prime shelf space in key locations. Maxim knew that these were critical for remaining competitive in the top stores, and was asking how Amy wanted these payments to be made: should he pay these bribes out of his own budget or was there a specific corporate budget dedicated for this purpose?

Amy was shocked! Coming from a smaller company with a far less global reach, Amy had never encountered a situation like this. But it was clear that this was how business was done in Moscow. What Amy quickly realized was that this behavior was not only inconsistent with her own ethical barometer, but it was also in conflict with her company's moral code, which explicitly forbade such illicit activities. Amy explained this to Maxim and decided that they would remain in the Moscow market, but have to find other, creative ethical ways of competing.

Professional Goals and the Decision to Adapt Cultural Behavior

Besides ethical and moral boundaries, another key consideration is whether adaptation will allow you to achieve your professional goals. In many cases it obviously does, but in some cases, it's not so certain.

Uli's Story: Coping with Habitual Tardiness

Uli Hermann was a German-born executive at a small IT company in India. Uli's challenge was how to cope with his local Indian employees who were consistently late for team meetings. When he first started at the company, Uli would arrive to meetings on time and would find himself the only person in the room—often for more than thirty minutes. Uli understood that there were cultural differences in orientation to time between India and Germany. The problem was that the global software industry was extremely fast-moving and competitive. Companies first to market typically had a major advantage in the workplace and Uli was extremely frustrated that his employees' local orientation toward time was putting the company at a global disadvantage.

One response would have been to relax his stricter standards and to accommodate the local approach. But Uli firmly believed that the Indian orientation toward time was putting the company at risk. He sometimes joked to himself that if this put the company out of business, his employees could then take all the time they needed when they were out of a job. Instead of switching behavior, therefore, Uli forced his employees to switch to *his* cultural style . . . but it wasn't easy. His subordinates protested, both overtly and also implicitly by refusing at first to accommodate to his standard. But over time, Uli did shape their behavior, and the result was very positive for the firm. The employees were far more timely in getting product to market and were able to maintain their competitive advantage.

Arlene's Story: The Benefits of Being Foreign

A similar story comes from Arlene O'Brien, an American-born executive coach living and working in Bangalore, who also occasionally makes the decision not to adapt her behavior because it's better for business. Arlene coaches local Indian managers and executives who are interested in fitting into Western companies operating in India. Although it helps that Arlene has a deep understanding of the Indian marketplace and a keen sensitivity to the cultural dynamics, it turns out that she has something else that her Indian clients cherish: her own foreignness. So, on certain occasions, when she senses that her clients are looking for a "Western" perspective, Arlene purposefully chooses not to switch behavior. For example, although she often dresses in Indian-style clothes, with certain clients she will wear a business suit to appear more Western and, in her clients' eyes, a more legitimate expert on the Western business world.

Arlene also chooses to maintain her own cultural behaviors when she feels that this would be effective. For example, she often acts more directly and assertively with her clients than she ever would if her goal were to accommodate the Indian norm. By acting outside the Indian zone of appropriateness, but in the context of a supportive coaching relationship, Arlene provides her clients with a realistic preview of an actual Western working environment, something that is initially uncomfortable, but that over time they learn to value. Is Arlene's behavior simply an excuse not to change? Not at all: it's actually a strategic use of her cultural style to make it fit her own goals as well as those of her clients. When she senses that an Indian approach is warranted, she certainly has that in her bag of cultural tricks. But by realizing when switching behavior is actually a liability, she can have a more nuanced approach toward cultural adaptation that enables her to achieve her professional goals on a more consistent basis.

Adapting Cultural Behavior Is a Choice

If adapting behavior helps you achieve your professional goals *and* you feel that it is not in conflict with your personal morals and ethics, then the choice to adapt behavior is likely a sensible option. This is not to say that you won't still experience psychological challenges switching behavior: you most likely will! You may very well feel inauthentic and frustrated and angry about having to adapt behavior to fit in and be effective. However, as you've seen in this chapter, this is quite different from an ethical breach where you feel that adapting to the new cultural norm is in deep violation of your personal morals and ethics. It's also possible that adapting will be less effective for your own goals—and those of the people you work with—than sticking with your native cultural behaviors. In the end, adapting cultural behavior is a choice that only you can make as you develop and hone your own global dexterity.

The Myth and Reality of Adapting Behavior across Cultures

We've covered a lot of territory in this book. We've discussed how you can develop your own global dexterity through diagnosis, customization, and integration of the new behavior into your personal repertoire. Along the way, we've met a chorus of professionals who have shared their stories and examples and have, I hope, taught you a thing or two about how to adapt your behavior across cultures.

Five Key Takeaways

Of the many valuable lessons you can find in these pages, table C-1 details what I believe to be the five key takeaways from this book. They all stem from the basic idea that when it comes to

TABLE C-1

Five key takeaways

Conventional wisdom	Reality
The key to successful cultural adaptation is learning about how another culture is different from yours.	The key to successful cultural adaptation is learning how to change your behavior to account for these differences.
You can't easily break your own cultural tendencies.	Your own cultural tendencies are more malleable than you imagine.
You don't have much, if any, leeway in another culture to behave as you want to behave.	You have far more leeway than you think to choose the way you'll behave in another culture.
Culture is a soft, squishy concept that is hard to define or assess.	You can clearly diagnose cultural style in six easy-to-understand and distinguishable dimensions.
You have to suppress your "true" nature when adapting to a foreign culture to be effective.	You can be yourself and be effective.

cultural adaptation, our conventional wisdom is misguided in several very important ways.

The most important takeaway is that the key to successful cultural adaptation is *not* merely learning about cultural differences—which is a lesson that you might mistakenly learn from reading most other books about culture. Don't get me wrong. Understanding cultural differences is clearly important. However, the reality is that global professionals don't just struggle with differences. Rather, they struggle with adapting their behavior in order to account for—and overcome—these cultural differences. That's a critical distinction, and the central purpose of this book has been to give you a set of tools to enable you to successfully switch your own cultural behavior. (And though we've explored those differences in the context of one national facing another culture, these tools can be used in more complex situations, when there is no clear path to follow.)

A related takeaway is that you have the power to change your behavior in a foreign culture from how you have always behaved to how you now know that you need to behave in order to fit in, be liked, and act effectively. The conventional wisdom holds that culture is relatively fixed and that you can't easily break or deviate from your own ingrained cultural routines; it also holds that culture is fixed in the other direction as well. In other words, you also don't have much, if any, leeway in *another* culture to behave as you want to.

What we have learned in this book is that you are *not* a prisoner of culture. You are actually a creative, empowered user of culture. Culture is more malleable than you might have thought, and you can adapt and deviate from your ingrained behaviors. Additionally, culture is also more malleable in the other direction. You have leeway to play with the other culture's rules for behavior, to sculpt them in a way that fits who you are and that is still appropriate in the new cultural setting. My hope here is that this new perspective about culture can feel empowering. Instead of focusing on differences, focus on how you can creatively, thoughtfully, and strategically manipulate your behavior to account for these differences, while at the same time staying true to yourself.

Another common belief that I hope this book debunks is that culture is a soft, squishy concept that is hard to define or assess. That may be true in some ways, but as you have seen here, the six-dimensional approach for classifying a cultural style is anything but squishy. Using this approach, you can adopt a hard, scientific lens for analyzing culture and, in doing so, have a very useful tool for learning how to successfully adapt and adjust your own behavior.

Finally, the last critical myth I hope I have exploded is that you have to suppress your true nature when adapting to a foreign culture to be effective. As the cases throughout this book have demonstrated, you can indeed be yourself and be effective at the same time. Adapting behavior is not about pure accommodation: it's about creative improvisation. It's about finding a way to creatively adjust how you behave so that you can create a compromise or hybrid version of behavior that achieves the best of both worlds. It's being personally comfortable while also being professionally effective.

These insights about culture have emerged from the stories of real professionals who have struggled and overcome the struggles of cultural adaptation, and in the spirit of storytelling, I'd like to tell one last story, and it's the story of someone you are already very familiar with. It's the story of Eric Rivers, with whom this book started. We know about the challenges that Eric faced, but we don't yet know about how he was able to resolve them.

How Eric Rivers Used Global Dexterity to Meet Cultural Challenges

When we left Eric, he was at a crossroads. He was a highly collaborative manager by nature, and almost by default brought this Western-style management approach to India, where it was failing miserably. His employees viewed his efforts to engage them as a weakness, and he was losing their trust and respect as a leader. Yet, although he understood what he needed to do to alter his behavior for this more authoritarian cultural environment, he strongly resisted; he just couldn't bear to treat employees in a way that he would never want to be treated himself. Let's see how Eric resolved the issues that he faced by using techniques similar to those described in the book.

Diagnosing the Source of the Cultural Conflict

Eric quickly realized that one of the key aspects of the cultural code that he was struggling with was the formality dimension. Participation is very formal in India. Employees just don't offer ideas the way they do in the United States. The boss is in charge and employees do what they are told to do. That's why Eric's employees interpreted his efforts to involve them more informally in the strategic decision-making process as a lack of confidence. Figure C-1 portrays this gap between the Indian style that characterized the approach and mentality of Eric's workers and his own personal comfort zone. As the figure shows, there is no zone of optimal performance for Eric—no place of overlap between how Eric feels comfortable behaving and what would be appropriate and effective in India.

FIGURE C-1

Eric's original situation

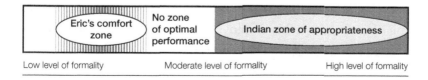

| Eric's comfort zone | No zone of optimal performance | Indian zone of appropriateness |

| Low level of formality | Moderate level of formality | High level of formality |

To feel comfortable in this situation, therefore, Eric needed to find a way to close this gap. He had to find a way to stretch himself so that he could operate beyond the relatively narrow comfort zone with which he was familiar. He did this in two ways. First, he worked on changing his perceptions of the behavior by internalizing the Indian cultural logic for the situation and by also embracing his own personal goals. These efforts helped him increase the size of his personal comfort zone to reach a point of intersection with the Indian cultural norms.

Customizing Perceptions of the Indian Cultural Code

As a first step in this process, he consulted with some close Indian colleagues as well as with a few trusted American colleagues who were longtime expatriates and quite familiar with the Indian cultural environment. From speaking with them, he learned to appreciate the Indian rules for hierarchy from an Indian cultural perspective. He learned how this focus on hierarchy is reflected and reinforced by norms at home, where the father is the traditional leader of the family and is recognized as the source of knowledge and authority. These same norms also characterize schools, where teachers as well are greatly respected and treated with high levels of deference, and corporate environments, where the boss is considered the ultimate authority. Seeing how this system was culturally ingrained, Eric was able to understand how, when experiencing him as a leader, his employees filtered his behavior through this hierarchical, authoritarian frame.

Understanding the Indian cultural perspective sensitized Eric to why his Indian employees behaved and reacted as they did. It also provided him with an understanding of how he would then be justified acting in a more authoritarian manner than he was used to in this new cultural context. It was what was expected and what was appropriate and justified in this setting.

In addition to internalizing the Indian cultural logic for the situation, Eric also embraced his own goals in the situation by revisiting the reasons he came to India in the first place and by reflecting on what he was hoping to achieve in his current managerial position. Eric had originally moved to India for a new challenge. He had become bored in his position in Los Angeles and was very enthusiastic about the fast-moving Indian market and about all the potential opportunities in this new technology frontier. He knew the cultural adaptation piece would be challenging, but one of his biggest goals in the process was to master the new cultural norms and to convince people that he could function effectively and be accepted as an Indian. He saw how foreign managers working in the United States were sometimes seen as effective, but not necessarily in the same league as native-born American managers. He wanted to be seen as simply effective in India, no matter his cultural origin. Revisiting these goals helped refocus his motivation on learning to adapt his cultural behavior. Although he did not initially understand the extent to which managing in India could potentially compromise his personal or cultural values, he was now determined to find some way that he could be effective while also being himself.

Creating a Fit Between Personal Style
and the New Cultural Code

This brings us to the second way in which Eric was able to reduce the level of identity conflict that he experienced: by shaping the way in which he performed the actual behavior. Recall that Eric was struggling to find a way of empowering workers while not losing their respect for him as a strong, confident leader. Employees were coming to him with strategic questions, and instead of offering a decisive solution, Eric would engage them in the process, asking them for their opinions on the problem in order to involve them and sharpen their own decision making skills. Although laudable from an American viewpoint, this style backfired in India, where employees expected their managers to be far more decisive, authoritarian leaders.

Eric ultimately came to understand and appreciate this cultural difference, but he still wanted to find a way to accommodate without losing himself in the process. His solution was to create a process that blended participation with hierarchy and formality. Whenever employees had strategic questions, they could come to him in a formal manner and he would authoritatively make a decision. However, there was a rule: in order to meet, employees had to develop three possible solutions on their own as well as a rationale for which of the three they would advocate as the best solution.

This protocol allowed Eric to have the best of both worlds. From the Indian standpoint, he was decisive and assertive, both in creating this rule and in enforcing it. For example, if someone had only thought of two solutions, he might require that person to go back and think of a third, plus offer a recommendation. Additionally, Eric would always be sure to be decisive in his ultimate decision once the three solutions and recommendations were presented to him, accommodating Indian expectations for firm and powerful leadership behavior. Moreover, this was a formal process, whereby he was requiring the workers to engage in a ritual. This emphasis on a formal requirement and a specific process for fulfilling the wishes of the leader was also consistent with the Indian cultural norms.

However, at the same time, this ritual also encouraged participation. It motivated workers to develop their own ideas, independent of his influence. This was very important for creating the atmosphere of bottom-up entrepreneurialism that Eric felt was so critical to effective management. Although it occurred through a process that was more formalized than would be typical in the United States, it ultimately achieved a similar purpose. In the end, Eric was able to craft behavior that accommodated Indian norms without losing who he was as a person and a leader.

Although in this particular case, rehearsal was not a big part of the story, evaluation certainly was. Eric was quite anxious to see how this would work, and the results were impressive. First of all was the sheer number of new ideas. Before instituting these policies, his employees would never offer a new idea. Now, Eric was getting many new ideas every day, along with very detailed and systematic analyses of the pros and cons. Second, not only was the company benefiting, but the employees were as well, by adding new skills to their personal repertoires. Additionally, over time, Eric's employees actually began to come to him less often, instead making and implementing decisions on their own. Eric was very pleased. He was able to stretch his own leadership style, help his employees adapt and grow, and strengthen the organization in the process. All in all: a successful cultural transformation.

———————

No one said that adapting your cultural behavior is easy. However, what I hope you have learned in this book is that it is possible, and that using the tools provided here, along with your own ingenuity, motivation, and courage, you can learn to adapt your own behavior across cultures on your own terms. I hope you will take the plunge.

Notes

Preface

1. Jack Welch, speech given to General Electric employees, 1997.

Chapter 2

1. To read more about the psychological challenges of adapting behavior across cultures, see A. L. Molinsky, "Cross-Cultural Code-Switching: The Psychological Challenges of Adapting Behavior in Foreign Cultural Interactions," *Academy of Management Review* 32 (2007): 622–640.

2. The Sergei story originally appeared in A. L. Molinsky, "Cross-Cultural Code-Switching" (unpublished PhD dissertation, Harvard University, 1999).

3. Note that with westernization of the Russian economy, some of these behaviors are changing, especially in Western firms operating in Russia.

4. G. Hofstede, *Cultures and Organizations: Software of the Mind* (Maidenhead, UK: McGraw-Hill, 1991).

5. Seating etiquette is very complicated in Japan, and there are many factors that determine where exactly the most important person at a meeting sits. However, in my research, I have found three things to be clear. First, it matters a great deal where people are seated, so take care if you are participating in a Japanese-style meeting to learn these rules from a local familiar with the protocol. Second, there does not appear to be an exact rule that applies to all Japanese meetings. The seating arrangements depend on many different factors, such as the configuration of the room, the mix of people in the audience, etc. This again makes it important to consult about your particular case ahead of time. Finally, one rule that does seem consistent across cases is that the most important or senior person in Japan does

not sit at the head of the table, as in the United States, and often will sit in the middle of the table—again, depending on the particular style of meeting and room configuration. This most important or senior person also sits as far as possible from the door to the room as a sign of honor and respect.

Chapter 3

1. Other factors can also influence the cultural code, such as functional differences (e.g., finance versus marketing), geographical differences (urban versus rural), generational differences, and so on. My aim is not to offer an exhaustive list, but to make the overall point that the cultural code is complex and can be influenced by multiple factors, with those in figure 3-1 being among the most obvious.

2. For additional information about high and low context cultures, see E. T. Hall, *Beyond Culture* (New York: Doubleday, 1976).

3. Of course, if Deepa were trained in the West or used to more Western norms from having lived or worked abroad, or even for a multinational company in India, she might have been more willing to offer direct feedback.

4. For more about power distance, see G. H. Hofstede, *Culture's Consequences: International Differences in Work-Related Values* (Beverly Hills, CA: Sage, 1980); and G. Hofstede, G. J. Hofstede, and M. Minkov, *Cultures and Organizations: Software of the Mind*, 3rd ed. (New York: McGraw-Hill, 2010). For another major research effort into understanding power distance and other cultural characteristics, see M. Javidan and R. J. House, "Cultural Acumen for the Global Manager: Lessons from Project GLOBE," *Organizational Dynamics* 29 (2001): 289–305.

5. In many cultures, for example, the younger generation does not exhibit the same cultural norms around power distance as the older generation, especially when interacting with each other. Also, in some countries, industry matters a great deal in influencing power distance. In China, for example, state-owned enterprises are more likely to reflect "traditional" Chinese cultural norms than western-owned businesses or smaller companies owned by expatriate Chinese.

Chapter 7

1. For a similar version of this diagram, along with an exercise for how to use it in training, see A. Molinsky, "A Situational Approach for Assessing and Teaching Acculturation," *Journal of Management Education* 34 (2010): 723–745.

Chapter 8

1. M. J. Gelfand, J. L. Raver, L. Nishii, L. M. Leslie, J. Lun, B. C. Lim, et al. "Differences Between Tight and Loose Cultures: A 33-Nation Study," *Science* 27 (2011): 1100–1104.

2. Ibid.

3. A. L. Molinsky, "Language Fluency and the Evaluation of Cultural Faux Pas: The Case of Russians Interviewing for Jobs in the United States," *Social Psychology Quarterly* 68 (2005): 103–120.

Chapter 10

1. This is a real example told to me by a western executive. However, when I presented this story to Indians, some of them mentioned that it feels a bit outdated, especially in the world of multinational corporations, where Indians typically conform to the multinational standards of these companies, which would likely encourage people to treat tea boys with politeness. Moreover, one Indian person I spoke with told me that the multinational company she worked for in India explicitly taught employees to be polite with everyone, irrespective of their positions in the company. Nevertheless, I include this example because it did happen, and it helps make the point that switching is indeed a choice.

Index

About the Author

Andy Molinsky is an associate professor of organizational behavior at Brandeis University's International Business School, with a joint appointment in the Department of Psychology. His experience working at a consulting firm in Paris in his early twenties inspired a deep interest in culture and cross-cultural adaptation, which he went on to pursue as part of a PhD degree at Harvard University focusing on psychology and organizational behavior.

Since that time, Molinsky has conducted a decade-long research program focusing on the challenges people experience when adapting behavior in a foreign culture and how they can successfully overcome them. His work has been published in top-tier scholarly journals in management, psychology, and sociology and has also been featured in media outlets such as the *Financial Times*, the *Boston Globe*, NPR, the Voice of America, *Harvard Business Review*, and the *Chronicle of Higher Education*. At Brandeis, he has created a popular MBA elective, Managing Across Cultures, and has also shared his insights with a wide range of audiences, including lawyers, judges, managers, teachers, consultants, bankers, university administrators, and academics. In addition to his PhD, he holds an MA in psychology from Harvard University, an MA in international affairs from Columbia University, and a BA in international affairs from Brown University.